National Wildlife Federation

Library of Congress CIP Data: page 95.

Ranger Rick's Holiday Book

Invitation to a Celebration

It's the Friday before Christmas and big flakes of snow are silently falling in Deep Green Wood. In the heart of the forest Ranger Rick and a few of his friends are meeting — to make some very important plans for the winter holidays.

"In just a few days we'll have our big party!" says Rick with a wide smile.

"Tooo-oo celebrate all our good times together," hoots Wise Old Owl.

"I *love* winter holidays!" cries Ollie Otter, zipping down a steep snowbank.

"And our party tops off our whole wonderful year!" sighs Becky Hare dreamily.

"This year," says Rick, chuckling, "getting *ready* for the party's going to be as much fun as the party itself!"

"How come, Rick?" asks Sammy Squirrel.

"Because this year," says Rick, "we're making a book all about winter holidays. It's our invitation to kids everywhere to join in the winter fun and come to our party!"

Wise Old Owl blinks one eye. "The more one knows about enjoyable times," she says,

4

"the more one enjoys them! In this book I'd like to share what *I* know about many different holiday traditions—where they come from and what they mean."

"*I'd* like to tell about nature's winter wonders," says Becky Hare.

Sammy scoops up some snow. "I'll show folks how to have lots of *fun* in winter!"

"Me, too," says Ollie. "I'll show how to make ornaments and toys and even holiday cookies that everyone will love to eat."

"Good ideas!" exclaims Rick. "Myself, I want to tell some stories that everyone will enjoy hearing on Christmas Eve."

"What's my part, Rick?" asks Cubby Bear, sort of snuffling.

"Why, Cubby," says Rick, "you have a very big job! You and Chester Chipmunk and Diggy Mole and Zelda Possum must find *all* our animal friends and invite them to the party!"

"This is the best holiday season ever!" pipes Chester, clapping his tiny paws.

Just then, from the woods, two snowballs zing at the group. Rick picks up one, Cubby the other. They whirl around to see Zelda and Sammy ducking behind two sturdy trees.

"It was Sammy's idea!" giggles Zelda.

"Aw, I was just showing you how to have lots of fun in winter," Sammy chuckles. "Anybody get hit?"

"No," says Rick, grinning, "—not *yet!* Let's get 'em, Cubby!"

PLOP! WHACK! The snowballs smash into the tree trunks. In a minute the air's full of flying snowballs and shrieks.

Finally Rick hollers, "Truce! Time to get busy on our holiday book!"

Off they all go, scampering away into the white, shadowy forest.

"See you soon!" they call to each other.

YOU'RE INVITED
We're having a party
On Christmas Day.
Just follow this map
And you'll find the way.
Wise Old Owl's
Holiday Traditions
Page 8
Becky Hare's
Winter Wonderland
Page 30

The Party!

Wise Old Owl's

Holiday Traditions

Whoo-oo doesn't know holiday traditions? What's Christmas without evergreen trees and Santa's reindeer? What's Hanukkah without candles? What's any holiday party without mistletoe hung in a doorway?

But do you know that near the North Pole where the reindeer live, every day's an adventure year round? I'm going to tell you a story about a reindeer herd and about one little calf and how it grew up.

I'm sure you know that if you stand under mistletoe you're apt to get kissed! But do you know what else this little green plant is famous for? A clue: Something magic!

You know how hard it is to pick just the *right* tree for Christmas. So many shapes! What different kinds! Know what the needles mean? I'll tell you! And I'll tell you too about Takashi and Kaya, who had no Christmas tree at all, in Japan, until. . . . Well, you shall see! And you'll see how David and Sarah, who had no Hanukkah candles, got help from a most unusual queen!

And, for toppers, I've made up a game about Christmas plants that you might find in your very own holiday garden.

8

Nomads of the Far North

The mother caribou was hurrying. Spring was coming, and her baby would soon be born. Along with ten other does, she was headed for the calving grounds on the northern Alaskan tundra, where the rich grasses grow.

All the does were carrying unborn calves. They had come almost five hundred miles across the snow-covered plains. They were thin, their ribs and hipbones stuck out, and their coats were worn. But their udders hung down, full of milk for the calves that would soon be born.

In North America caribou live on all the lands around the North Pole. Their partly domesticated relative, the reindeer, is found in Asia and Europe. But these two animals are so much alike that scientists call them all by the same name, *Rangifer tarandus*.

Because caribou and reindeer live in the frigid north, they have thick, furry coats to protect them from the cold weather. Even their noses are covered with fur—and long hollow guard hairs protect most of their bodies. These hairs are filled with air. So when a caribou swims, the hairs serve as a kind of life

jacket to help keep the animal from sinking.

Caribou have large, splayed feet that act as snowshoes to help them walk on the snow in winter and over the boggy tundra in summer. Both the bucks (the males) and the does (the females) have antlers that begin to grow in spring and are not fully developed until fall.

Weeks after their journey began, the does reached their calving grounds near the Arctic Ocean. Here spring was coming. The ice was breaking up, the plants were pushing through the melting snow. Millions of birds were arriving to nest. Voles and lemmings, wolves and foxes, weasels and hares, all had homes full of wriggling babies.

A few days after the caribou arrived, the lead doe gave birth to her calf in a snowdrift. She licked him dry and urged him onto his feet. Soon he was drinking his first meal from her milk-filled udder. The rich milk helped the calf grow fast. On the second day, he could run after his mother. By the third day, he could run as fast as she did. In ten days he had doubled his birth weight of thirteen pounds.

The sun blazed down both day and night in this northern land. At the peak of summer there are twenty-four hours of daylight and none in the middle of winter. The snow was melting faster every day, and green plants and flowers were sprouting hourly from the tundra.

The mother doe wandered slowly from place to place, the little calf close beside her. Picking out the best plants to eat, she nipped off the new, delicate shoots. She ate grasses and sedges, willow and larch. But she would not touch heath or globeflower. Caribou are fussy eaters.

The calf's mother also liked to wander along the seashore, where she ate salty strands of seaweed washed up by the Arctic waves. Sometimes she found a dead fish among the seaweed and ate that too.

The calf watched what his mother ate. Now and then he took a bite of a tender plant or berry (3) but mostly he lived on her rich milk. Soon he was playing with the other calves on the tundra.

Now the caribou bucks joined the herd. They came north later than the does. They were larger than the calf's mother, and they had much bigger antlers.

In the days that followed, the sun no longer stayed above the horizon all the time. Twilight became longer, and soon there were even short periods of night. Birds and animals that cannot live in the Arctic winter prepared to migrate, or journey south.

The deep Arctic snow makes it difficult for caribou to find food in winter, so they have to migrate back to the forest regions. There the trees protect them against the fierce winter winds and they can find enough vegetation to eat.

Before the first flurries of autumn snow the caribou began their journey, following a migration route that has been used for centuries. Other herds of caribou joined them along the way.

After a few days they came to a wide river with a swift current (4). The calf was separated from his mother, but he kept swimming until he staggered out on the other side. Then he stood on the beach

1

2

Caribou (1) nibble a mouthful of food here and a bit there, but nothing really stops their journey north. Some of their calves are born along the way. But as soon as a baby is on its feet, the march goes on.

A newborn calf (2) rests for a moment on the snow before joining the herd.

and howled until his mother found him.

The migration went on. The herd crossed the tundra and the mountains, the rivers and the lakes.

After several weeks the caribou came to the first trees they had seen on their journey south. They went on until they found a thick forest where they would still be able to find food during the winter.

In the forest the caribou rubbed their antlers against the trees to scrape off the "velvet," or outside skin, and to sharpen the horn underneath. The bucks would use their antlers as weapons in the battles that determined their position in the herd.

Soon not a day passed without a duel of strength. The fighting bucks put their heads down and ran together (5),

clashing antlers, snorting and roaring. They pushed and pushed, each trying to force the other backwards or down to the ground.

Finally, two or three of the strongest bucks were able to drive the others away. The victorious bucks collected a number of does and herded them off. The calf's mother went with the strongest buck. They stayed together in a

group and the buck mated with each doe.

Soon fall turned to winter in the northern lands. It was a time of cold and darkness. The days grew even shorter until the sun no longer rose above the horizon. The caribou moved deeper into the forest to find more food.

Winter is not a hardship for the caribou because they know how to live in snow. The calf learned how to dig for plants with his sharp hooves. He found wintergreen and cranberry and even some marsh grass.

At last winter passed, and the does began to act nervous. It was time for them to migrate north again to the calving grounds. In a few months their calves would be born, and they had five hundred miles to travel.

The calf was now a young buck who didn't need his mother anymore. He and the other young males would stay with the older bucks now and do what they did. When the leaders went north, they followed, memorizing by sight and smell the route northward. In a few years, when it was the young buck's turn to lead the herd, he would be ready.
ALICE L. HOPF

Mistletoe Magic

Long ago, people worshiped mistletoe. They believed that a spirit from heaven lived in its green branches. How else could a plant grow on a dead-looking, leafless tree? It had to be magic!

The Druids were priests in Britain, France and Ireland 2,000 years ago. They thought that mistletoe was the symbol of a spirit because it had no roots in the earth. They held their religious ceremonies under large oak trees on which mistletoe grew.

Other people had the idea that mistletoe had powers to help the sick and dying. They thought that any house in which mistletoe hung was free from witchcraft.

Early Christians believed mistletoe to be a link between heaven and earth because it grew in trees and never touched the ground.

Some ancient tribes thought mistletoe was the plant of peace. Under its "sacred" green branches the Scandinavians met with their enemies and settled their quarrels. From this tradition of truce may have come our custom of kissing beneath the mistletoe.

Since those early times we have learned much about how plants live. Most plants grow and make their own food by adding together air and water and minerals from the soil with the help of sunlight. But some plants steal food or water and minerals from other plants. These plants attach themselves to other living plants, or "hosts," as the victims are called. Such uninvited guests are called parasites.

Mistletoe is a parasite. It produces sticky seeds which sprout on the branches of trees. There the tiny roots pierce the bark of the limb. Then they take the water and minerals the mistletoe needs.

Birds help spread mistletoe from tree to tree. Its seeds grow inside small white berries that are tasty to birds. Perhaps a seed that is sticking to a bird's bill will be wiped off onto the bark of another tree. Or when a bird eats the berries, the seeds pass through the bird and may fall on a tree limb in the bird's droppings. Mistletoe berries are very good eating for birds, but are *very* poisonous to humans.

There are many kinds of mistletoe in North America. It is most common in the warm southern and western states. Some kinds grow into thick, leafy, evergreen balls.

Mistletoe has tiny yellowish flowers which bloom in October or November. The small berries which soon follow are filled with a sticky, almost clear pulp.

Mistletoe is a traditional Christmas decoration that is still used today. It's true that we no longer take the old beliefs about the plant too seriously. Yet most of us still like to keep the old custom of kissing beneath a sprig of mistletoe.

FAY VENABLE

A Christmas Garden

Christmas just wouldn't seem like Christmas without colorful holiday plants. Carolers sing about "The Holly and the Ivy," and storytellers recall the legend of the Christmas rose. And who has not seen flower shops filled with glorious red poinsettias?

These plants, and others too, do more than just decorate our stores and homes. Some are supposed to tell stories—stories about the first Christmas and about miracles that happened during the holidays.

Here is a Christmas garden of pictures where six of these plants are growing: *holly, ivy, laurel, poinsettia, rosemary* and *Christmas rose.*

But which is which? Read the stories at right for clues, and see if you recognize the plants from their descriptions. Then match the pictures with the stories.

You may not know all of the plants since some are not as familiar in the United States as they are in Europe. But the legends that have grown up around many of them add meaning to the winter holiday season. You'll find the answers upside down at the bottom of the next page.

1 According to one legend, this plant was created on the very first Christmas. Among the visitors to Bethlehem was a young girl, sad because she had no gift. Tears of disappointment fell from her face. Where they touched the ground, a bush grew—and on it was her gift, a white, roselike flower. This is a true Christmas plant, for it blooms in winter.

2 The Greeks used branches of this plant to make wreaths to crown the heads of their heroes. Romans used it for decoration at their December Saturnalia festival. Later it was adopted for Christmas use as well. Today this plant is most common in the kitchen, where it's used as the spice called bay leaf.

3 This evergreen shrub, once a popular Christmas decoration, is another food seasoning. Its legend also goes back to the time of the first Christmas. While on the flight into Egypt, Mary washed her baby's clothes and hung them on this bush to dry. Ever since, according to tradition, its leaves have had a mild, pleasant smell.

4 The newest plant in our garden, this red favorite is from Mexico. Our ambassador there brought it to the U.S. over 150 years ago. The legend it recalls may sound familiar: a poor girl on her way to church had no gift to offer. She took the only present she could find, weeds growing by the road. When placed on the altar, they turned into flowers.

5 This green vine is a common sight creeping up aging brick walls and across fences. But in some places it is also a popular Christmas green. Even when cut for decoration, the vine stays green through the holidays. Its leaves are thick, with waxy coatings, so they don't dry out too quickly.

6 Druids believed that this plant stayed green year-round so the world would be beautiful after other trees lost their leaves. Later, Christians adopted it as a Christmas symbol. With its bright berries and leaves, this plant may have started our custom of using red and green as Christmas colors.
VICTOR WALDROP

A

E

B

C

D

F

ANSWERS:
(1-E) Christmas rose: (2-C)
Laurel; (3-D) Rosemary;
(4-A) Poinsettia;
(5-F) Ivy; (6-B) Holly.

The Forever Christmas Tree

It was December in Sugi Village high in the hills of Japan. Already the first snow had covered the land, and the fields looked cold and bleak. Now the days were short and the nights were long, and it was the quiet time of the year.

It was also a lonely time, especially for a little boy named Takashi who lived at the edge of the village. There were no more persimmons for him to pick or mushrooms to hunt. There was nothing at all to do now but wait for the New Year, and that seemed far away.

If only I had someone to play with, Takashi thought. If only I had a friend next door.

Their only neighbor, however, was an old man whose name was Mr. Toda and who seemed as old as forever. His face was covered with wrinkles, and he had a long, thin beard as white as an egret's breast.

Mr. Toda did not have any friends either. He thought people were a bother so he lived alone, reading his books and tending his garden.

But deep down in his heart, Mr. Toda longed for a friend to talk with during the lonely days of his old age.

Mr. Toda knew, of course, that there was a little boy named Takashi next door. But he had no time for little boys. They were a nuisance, and he had put up a tall hedge around his garden to keep them all out.

One day when it was too cold to play outside, Takashi sat where he could watch for his sister Kaya to come home from school. When at last he saw her, she was running, and Takashi knew she had something special to tell. As soon as she was in the house, the words came tumbling out.

"Today we learned about Christmas!" she said, and the bright glow of her excitement quickly spilled out to fill Takashi too.

Takashi did not know about Christmas for no one celebrated it in Sugi Village. It was the New Year that mattered.

She told him about the very first Christmas in Bethlehem, and she told about the wisemen and the shepherds who traveled to see the baby Jesus. Then, at the very last, she told him about Christmas trees with their lights and colored balls and strings of candy.

Takashi listened hard with his whole body. When Kaya finished, he closed his eyes, and he could see a Christmas tree all covered with decorations. From that moment Takashi wanted a Christmas tree more than anything else.

18

The next day Takashi went outside with his dog, Shiro, and looked at the trees around their house. There were gnarled pine trees, leafy trees, and barren trees, but none that looked anything at all like a Christmas tree.

Just when Takashi thought he would never find a Christmas tree, Shiro did something to help him. Shiro saw a rabbit run under Mr. Toda's hedge and bounded away after it.

Old Mr. Toda would beat Shiro with a stick if he caught him, Takashi thought. He ran to the hedge, got down flat on his stomach, and peered through the hole that Shiro had wriggled through. The old man was nowhere in sight and neither was Shiro. Takashi sighed with relief and was about to get up when he saw a beautiful little fir tree planted in a wooden tub. The wind had knocked it over, and the tree was crooked. But even so Takashi could tell it was a perfect Christmas tree. All it needed were some trimmings.

Takashi told Kaya about the little fir tree in Mr. Toda's yard.

"Help me," he said to her. "I want it for a Christmas tree."

"Surely we cannot have the old man's tree," she said, "but let's make some decorations anyway. We can hang them on the branches of our pine tree."

Kaya got out scissors and paste and her box of special papers. Together they cut and pasted many, many loops and linked them together in one long chain. They folded golden storks and silver balloons. And they made boats and birds from the lovely colored squares of paper.

"On the day that is called Christmas Eve," Kaya said, "we can hang these on our pine tree."

Takashi nodded, but he was thinking how much better they would look on the old man's little fir tree.

Early the next morning Takashi crept softly to the hedge and looked for the fir tree. But the tree was not where it had been before. The old man had planted it beside his front entrance, and now it would stand there sturdy and firm forever. Takashi hung his head. He could no longer dream about having the tree.

On December twenty-fourth Kaya came home rosy cheeked from the cold and the excitement that bubbled inside her.

"Today is the day that is called Christmas Eve," she said to Takashi. "Tonight we will decorate our pine tree."

So that night Kaya and Takashi bundled themselves up and carried their decorations outside. They went to the foot of the pine tree and looked up at it.

"We have only enough decorations for one branch of this big tree," Kaya said sadly.

Kaya and Takashi stood for a moment in the icy coldness of the winter night. Then, without saying anything to each other, they began to walk toward Mr. Toda's house.

"Shall we just see how it looks?" Kaya asked. "Just for a minute?"

Takashi knew what she meant. It was what he wanted to do too. Together they hurried in the darkness toward the old man's fir tree.

Then, without a word, they took out their colored paper trimmings and decorated the little tree.

When they stepped back to look at it, Kaya clasped her hands together and said, "It is the most beautiful Christmas tree in the whole wide world."

Even after many minutes they still could not make themselves take down the trimmings.

Takashi spoke in a whisper. "Do you think Mr. Toda would be mad if we left it just for one day?"

Kaya thought for a moment and then she smiled. "I do not think he will be angry, Takashi," she said. "Maybe . . . maybe . . . if he can be filled with Christmas too, he will even like it just a little."

So they took one last look and then ran home.

The next morning Mr. Toda was up at dawn. He slid open the door and blinked at the sun. It made brilliant patterns of light on the snow, and the old man blinked again. Even his little fir tree seemed covered with bright colors. He stepped closer and bent down to inspect it.

At that moment Takashi came to look at the tree. He peered around the hedge and suddenly he was looking right at Mr. Toda.

"Come here," the old man beckoned. "Do you know who did this to my tree?"

At last Takashi nodded. "I . . . I . . . I . . .," he said in a small voice. "Kaya and I did it. It's . . . it's a Christmas tree."

Takashi was so frightened, he was ready to run home. But as he turned to go he bumped into Kaya who had come with Mother and Father.

"I am sorry our children trimmed your tree without permission," Father said solemnly.

"They should have spoken to you first," Mother added. "I hope they did no harm."

20

But even as they spoke they had to smile, for the Christmas tree looked so bright and cheerful standing in the snow.

The old man nodded as though he agreed with every word they said. Then slowly, the crooked curve of a smile crept over his face.

"It is the first time in my life that I have had a Christmas tree," he said.

"Then you are not angry?" Kaya asked.

The old man shook his head. "You have not harmed the tree," he answered.

"Would it be all right if I showed my friends?" Kaya asked. Without waiting for an answer she ran down the road to the village. Takashi followed her as she ran from house to house, calling to all the other children.

Big children and small children, boys and girls came from all over the village to see the wonderful tree. The children looked and looked at the old man and the tree, for both were new and wonderful sights. Everyone felt good inside, even the old man. He said to Takashi, "You may trim the tree next year too."

"And the year after that?" Takashi asked.

The old man nodded. "Every Christmastime," he said.

"Forever?" Takashi asked.

The old man nodded again. "For as long as you like."

Takashi thought he would burst with joy.

Gradually, one by one, everyone went home. But Takashi and Kaya could not stay away for very long. They came back again and again to add more decorations.

The old man came to watch the children for he, too, found it hard to stay away from the tree. And as he watched, he knew that for the first time in many, many months, he was no longer sad. He knew that he had not only found Christmas, but a great deal more.

"Come, Takashi," Kaya said at last. "We must go home now."

Takashi took one more look at the tree, and said happily, "Our forever Christmas tree!"

Then he waved to Mr. Toda and the old man raised his hand in return.

As Takashi walked home, a grin spread slowly over his face, for suddenly he realized that at last something exciting had happened to him. He had discovered Christmas and he had found a new friend. He had waited a long, long time, but in the twelfth month, this year had become a very special one indeed.

YOSHIKO UCHIDA

Your Christmas Tree

Nature comes into our homes many times during the year: pussy willows in spring, daisies in summer, colored leaves in autumn, and an evergreen tree at Christmastime.

But why an evergreen? This custom goes back thousands of years into pre-Christian history. It was believed that evergreen trees stood for eternal life.

Today, we still celebrate with evergreens. They just naturally go with Christmas—

like snow and reindeer—don't they? One Christmas you may have a Scotch pine. The next you may want to try a spruce, fir or juniper.

Do you know how to identify the different Christmas trees? It's easy. Look at the needles on your tree. If they are gathered into little bundles or groups of two, three or five, you have a pine (1). Does each needle grow on the branch by itself? Then your tree is a fir or a spruce, but you'll

have to look closely to tell which it is. Do you see two white lines on the underside of each needle? If so, the tree is a fir (2). If not, then you have a spruce (3). Spruce needles are sharply pointed.

What? Your tree is not any of these? Then I'll bet it has very tiny needles, so small they look almost like fish scales. If it looks like that, you have a juniper (4)! Junipers may also have little blue-green cones that look a lot like berries. If your tree is a red cedar species of juniper, notice the red and white wood where it was cut.

When it is time to take down your Christmas tree, examine the cut end. See the rings? Each ring represents a year's growth. If the tree has not been clipped to improve its shape, or injured in some way, you may find as many annual rings as there are layers of branches.

What other stories can we read in the rings? If the rings are wide near the center of the stem and then get narrower and narrower toward the bark, your tree might have grown in a Christmas tree plantation. As the trees around it grew, they crowded your tree so it grew less each year. Or it might mean there was not enough rain. If the rings get wider near the bark, that could mean growing conditions improved.

There are fun things to do with your tree after Christmas. We poke ours into a hole in the ground to shelter the winter birds. On the branches we hang strings of popcorn and cranberries, pine cones dipped in melted suet, and little mesh onion bags containing pieces of suet.

You might even arrange your tree and two others from neighbors into a group so that their inner branches touch. Sparrows, juncos and others will use them for sleeping and as shelters from winter storms.

Is your Christmas tree a fir? If so, you have still another treat in store. Crush some needles and smell them. The scent reminds me of cool forests. Now try this: Put some fir needles in a small cloth bag and hang it in your closet for months of wonderful fragrance.

Your Christmas tree can bring nature to your home all year round.
RICHARD B. FISCHER

1

PINES
Long, round needles growing in clusters make pines easy to identify. Scotch pine is now America's favorite Christmas tree.

2

FIRS
These make good indoor Christmas trees because they are well-shaped and hold their needles a long time after being cut.

3

SPRUCES
These hardy favorites, especially the blue and black spruces, grow in cooler areas where they are often decorated outdoors.

4

JUNIPERS
This red cedar, a type of juniper, has a natural Christmas ornament—berries containing seeds. Birds also feed on the berries.

A Season to Celebrate

December brings days that are short and cold. But the month also brings many holidays that brighten our spirits. Two holidays in particular, Hanukkah and Santa Lucia Day, really do brighten up the season—since candles are part of these celebrations. Saint Nicholas, known as Santa Claus to us, also brings cheer at this time of the year, but on different days in different parts of the world.

SAINT NICHOLAS DAY

Saint Nicholas was a church leader who lived 16 centuries ago. The Dutch called him Sinterklaas, a name we in the U.S. have turned into Santa Claus. According to stories still told today, he performed many miracles and even gave a gift of gold to three poor sisters.

In this country we expect him to visit children on Christmas Eve. But in many parts of Europe, he has his own special time, the eve of December 6.

In Switzerland there is a celebration in his honor that night. People parade through the streets wearing tall hats lighted from inside by candles (1). These hats are called Yffeln (IF-feln), and look like the hats worn by some church leaders. Large Yffeln may be six feet high and weigh 40 pounds. With their cutout designs they look like cathedral windows.

Later that night, Saint Nicholas himself visits families at dinnertime. He brings cookies and fruit. He also warns naughty children that if they want to get Christmas presents later on, they must mend their ways.

SANTA LUCIA DAY

Santa Lucia Day is celebrated in Sweden on December 13. Lucia was a saint in the third century A.D. who chose death rather than marry a pagan. Today she is honored by young girls who dress up like her, with white robes, red sashes and crowns of candles (2). Lucia would carry food to the hungry, so the girls keep up that tradition. But nowadays they serve their families, with bread, cakes and coffee. Everyone tries to finish all holiday plans—even buying presents—by Santa Lucia Day. They also prepare the Christmas dish, lutfisk (LOOT-fisk), burying a boiled fish in ashes in preparation for Christmas dinner.

HANUKKAH

Hanukkah is called the Feast of Lights. It celebrates the victory of Judas Maccabeus and his Jewish followers in Palestine—today's Israel— 2,100 years ago. After driving their enemies from Jerusalem, the Jews were able to return at last to their holy Temple. When the time came to light the Temple's sacred lamp, there was enough oil for only one night. But by a miracle, this oil lasted for eight days. By then a fresh supply could be obtained. So today in December, Jews around the world celebrate that miracle and the return to the Temple. They burn candles in nine-branch holders (3) called menorahs (muh-NOR-ahs), lighting one candle a night for eight nights. The ninth candle is used to light the others.
VICTOR WALDROP

1

2

3

Bee-utiful Candles

The characters in this story, the Pitzels, are tiny, imaginary people who are preparing for the real Jewish holiday of Hanukkah.

The Pitzel-sailors had forgotten to get Hanukkah candles, and now, with Hanukkah only one day away, there wasn't a single Hanukkah candle anywhere in Pitzel-land!

All the Pitzels were sad, of course, but saddest of all were the children. They could hardly eat breakfast that morning, and when they left their snug little houses under the strawberry bushes, they couldn't think of playing. In fact, all David and his sister Sarah and their friends could think of doing was to sit in the shade of some flowers and poke the ground with their feet.

A hummingbird was watching them. He didn't know why they were sad, but he didn't care. "Pitzel children should always be laughing," he said to himself, "and in a minute they will be!" Then he darted over and began flying around their heads—backwards! The Pitzels all laughed out loud. All except one, because David wasn't laughing. He wasn't even smiling. He was listening.

Suddenly David jumped up—the hummingbird's hum had reminded him of something.

"Bees!" he shouted. "And bees make wax. We can get wax from the bees and make our own Hanukkah candles!"

"Not so fast," said the hummingbird. "If you want wax from the bees, you'll have to ask their queen for it, and from what I've heard about her, you'll never get it."

"Anyway, we've got to try—it's our only chance," said David. "What's the queen's name, hummingbird?"

"Let's see, I knew her name once . . . Mellifica; yes, that's it—Queen Mellifica!"

"All right, Queen Mellifica—here I come!"

"Wait for me!" Sarah called after him as he started off. And hand in hand, brother and sister walked down the path to the hollow tree where the bees lived.

Now Queen Mellifica really wasn't a bad queen, no matter what the hummingbird had heard. But she did have her "bad days," and, unluckily for David and Sarah, this was one of them. So when the Lord of the Queen-bee Chamber came to tell her that two Pitzels were outside the hive waiting to see her, she almost flew off her throne, crying out:

"Impossible, impossible! You know very well, Lord Apis, that today is one of my bad days! I'm in no condition to see anyone!"

"Forgive me, Your Majesty," Lord Apis quietly answered, "but I think you should see them. You need a little cheering up, and the Pitzels are—well, they're so funny. You never leave the hive, and so you cannot know what funny creatures there are in this world."

"Funny? In what way are the Pitzels funny?"

"Well, first of all," Lord Apis went on, "they have no wings—they have to walk all the time! As if that weren't enough, the poor things have only four legs, instead of six. But the funniest part of all is, they walk on only two of their legs, while the other two just hang!"

"Enough!" laughed the queen. "If what you say is true, have them brought to the throne room immediately!"

Lord Apis hurried to the entrance of the hive to tell David and Sarah that the queen had graciously consented to see them. Then he ordered one of the drone bees to fly them up to her chamber.

David and Sarah mounted on the drone's back and up they went. At last they reached the highest point of the hive, the throne room itself, shining in a blaze of gold!

Standing now in the presence of the queen, David made a real bow, while Sarah curtsied to the floor. They stayed that way, waiting for the queen to speak. But it took some time for the queen to speak. The Pitzels seemed even funnier than Lord Apis had described them.

Finally, she controlled herself and said:

"Why have you come? Tell me quickly, for I must get my rest. Yesterday, you see, I laid 4,281 eggs! So come to the point—what is it you want?"

David cleared his throat. "Wax, Your Majesty. We Pitzels need wax."

"Wax?! Whatever for? I can see you don't live in a hive, so why would you need wax?"

"For candles," David replied.

"And what are candles?" the queen asked. "What do you do with them?"

"Burn them, Your Majesty."

"Burn them? Then what is left of the wax?"

"Why . . . nothing!" David said.

"NOTHING?" Queen Mellifica could hardly believe what she was hearing. "You mean you'll take my good wax and make it into things called candles only in order to burn them up until there's nothing left? In other words, you want my wax—for nothing! . . . Well, this must be some kind of Pitzel joke. I assure you, we are not amused."

"Oh please, Your Majesty," David cried out. "We do want your wax for something, something very important. You don't understand about candles. You see, when the sun goes down tomorrow we Pitzels start celebrating our holiday of Hanukkah. Hanukkah is a wonderful, a beautiful holiday—but only if there are candles. Hanukkah is even called the Feast of Lights! It lasts for eight days, and each day we light one more candle until, on the last day, the special candlestick is full. And while the candles burn and their flames dance in the air, they make us think of the time when our freedom and our Temple were won back for us by the good, the magnificent Maccabees—"

"*Macca*-bees, *macca*-bees?" interrupted the queen. "I've never heard of *those* bees before, though I dare say they're distant relatives of ours—*we* are honeybees, you know. . . . Well now, that's a completely different story! If those candles of yours make you think of bees —macca or any other kind—they *are* important for you to have! In that case, you're welcome to the wax."

David and Sarah began shouting: "Thank you, thank you!" but the queen quieted them. "Please, please, I have a head-buzz as it is. Now then, my workers will spend the rest of the day filling up on honey and they'll be ready with your wax tomorrow morning. Where shall I send them?"

"To the Star of David Lake, Your Majesty," David said. "Uncle Ben has his workshop there. He's a sculptor; he'll know how to make your wax into candles."

Queen Mellifica nodded. Then slowly, with great dignity, she rose up from her throne and began flying out of the room. Just before she left, however, she said to herself—loud enough for David and Sarah to hear:

"The macca-bees may well have been as brave as those Pitzels say. But I wonder if *their* queen ever laid 4,281 eggs in a single day!"

LEONARD JAFFE

Becky Hare's

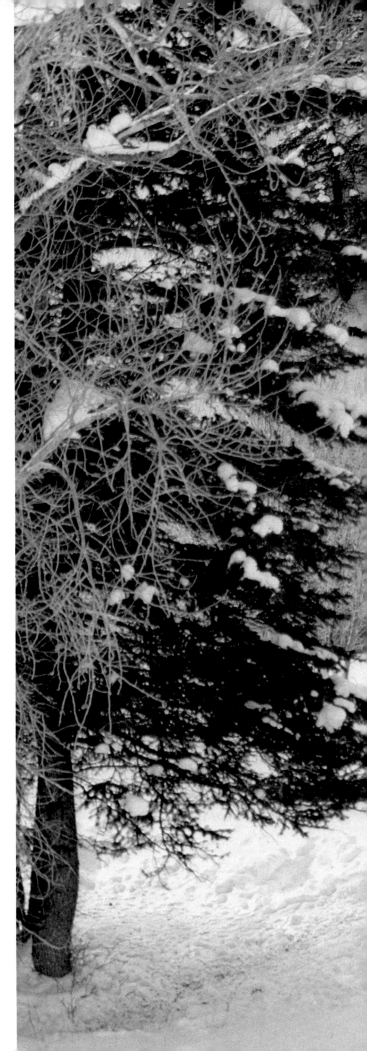

Winter Wonderland

When the air's cold and the wind blows, and snow makes your backyard look like the top of a fluffy, white-frosted birthday cake, do you wonder: What *is* it—snow?! How is it made? Why isn't it rain? Is it true that no two snowflakes are alike? Well, I'm going to tell about snow—and all the good things it does for us. And I have some great stories about frozen "monsters" that have been buried for thousands of years.

Isn't wintertime wonderful? Lots of us like the cold, don't we! (And lots of us don't!) Animals have so many ways to keep nice and warm! It's amazing—the way nature tells us whether to go south, to go to sleep for months at a time, or just to grow thicker coats when winter comes! It all depends on who we are, where we live. Wait till you read about a speckled brown bird and the trouble he got into trying to keep warm!

If you like winter as much as I do, you have probably dreamed about living up at the North Pole. Polar bears love it there. So does the Eskimo boy, Naput—except when he's chased by a bear! *That's* some story—wonderful, and a little bit wild!

Snow

It is snowing! Last night the moon shone dimly through a silvery overcast. This morning, clouds covered the entire sky with a dull, gray sheet. And now, in the middle of the afternoon, the clouds are low. Snowflakes have begun to float quietly down. The day is not very cold; it is just above freezing. The snow is rather wet and the flakes are large. Good packing snow! Good snow for snowballs and snowmen!

There is a sudden cold touch on your cheek. A snowflake has come in for a landing. In the space of a second it is melted to a drop of water by the warmth of your skin. You look up and catch flakes on your eyelashes. Suddenly you feel surrounded by the magic of snow!

The snowflakes that fell on your clothes appear to be exquisite little stars with feathery branches. These lovely flakes belong to the largest family of snowflakes: the stellar type. There are other types of snowflakes that you can learn to recognize with a magnifying glass or even with your naked eye. Some of the most common ones are plates, which look like flat, six-sided dinner plates, and plates-with-extensions.

Even within one type of snowflake, the individual flakes are not alike. In fact, it's probable that no two snowflakes have ever been exactly alike among all the countless billions that have fallen since the first snowflake fluttered to earth millions of years ago.

Snow is formed when the right combination of temperature and moisture exists in storm clouds. First, water in the form of gas, or water vapor, is carried by the air into the cold upper atmosphere. At the same time, warm air filled with small bits of dust rises from the earth. If the temperature in the clouds is above freezing (0° C), the water vapor will form droplets around the particles of dust and fall as rain. But in winter, the clouds are often freezing or below, so the water vapor freezes on the bits of dust and ice crystals begin to grow.

What form a snowflake will take, how large it will be when it finally falls to earth, and how much delicate design it will have depend upon the weather conditions in the clouds where it is born. For instance, one day may not be very cold; the clouds will be low, fairly warm, and full of moisture; so the flakes will be mostly the stellar type.

Another day, however, the temperature may be very low and the clouds high and rather dry. The snowfall from these clouds will not be as heavy as from warmer, wetter clouds. The flakes will probably be small six-sided plates, or six-sided plates with feathery arms growing from the corners.

Stellar flakes are starlike with six branched plumes.

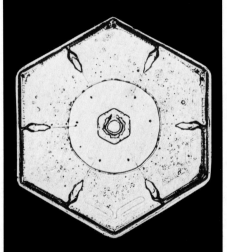

Hexagonal plates are thin, flat flakes made of solid ice.

Plates-with-extensions have broad crystals at each corner.

Snow seems light and weightless as it floats down. You would probably laugh if someone asked you to weigh a snowflake, yet the weight of snow covering an acre of ground would make you gasp. And no wonder! A 10-inch snowfall over an acre of land weighs about 113 tons!

If it's your job to clean the sidewalk after a blizzard, you may be shoveling quite a cloudful of tiny snowflakes. Suppose your sidewalk measures 50 feet by 5 feet, and that the snow is dry and fluffy and 15 inches deep. Not counting the weight of the shovel, by the time you have completely cleaned the walk you will have lifted close to 1,950 pounds, or nearly a ton of snow. (A 15-inch dry fluffy snow weighs about the same as an 8-inch moist snow because dry snow has a lot more air in it.)

A heavy blanket of snow is quiet and peaceful on level ground. It is welcomed by both farmers and gardeners. In the fall, frost comes as a plowman to loosen and break up the soil. Then snow falls to cover the ground with a soft mulch. This serves the same purpose as a covering of leaves or straw on flower gardens that have been put to bed for the winter.

You might think that snow would make too cold a coverlet for plants. On the contrary, snow in bitter winter weather keeps plants alive, because the air is warmer under the snow than above it.

While snow on level ground is quiet, snow on steep slopes can be dangerous. It is restless, unstable, ready to take off down a mountainside the moment the right conditions arise. The right conditions for a mountain snowslide may be a thaw, a thaw followed by a sudden freezing, or a heavy snowfall on top of a deep layer of snow.

You know what happens when a house roof is covered with snow and a thaw occurs. On the sun-warmed slope of the roof, water trickles down to the shingles, running under the snow and providing a fine lubricant. Suddenly the whole sheet of snow lets go and slides off the roof to the ground with a loud plop.

Great sheets of snow clinging to mountain slopes let go in the same way and become roaring avalanches that can bury buildings and people alike. Not only are the masses of hurtling snow destructive, but the air blast that is pushed ahead of the avalanche can destroy anything in its path. There is also a strong vacuum at the rear of the avalanche that sucks in every object on the sides of its path.

An avalanche like the one in this picture can travel faster than a train. It can speed down a mountain, cross a valley, rush up the slope of a mountain on the other side, and return to the valley in a matter of minutes.

Beautiful, often helpful, sometimes destructive, every year snow keeps a covering of white over one-fifth of the earth's surface.

THELMA HARRINGTON BELL

What Do You Know About Snow?

You know snow is cold. But did you know snow is also warm? In bitter-cold snowy weather, chickadees, bob-whites, ruffed grouse, and snow buntings dive right into a snowbank to get warm!

Snow becomes a cozy blanket because of the still air trapped in it. The temperature of the ice crystals near the ground stays around freezing. So the snowbank insulates animals and plants from colder weather outside.

HOW WARM IS SNOW?

MEASURING AIR IN SNOW

MEASURING SNOWFALL

You can find out how warm a blanket of snow is by testing it with a thermometer. First take a reading of the air temperature and write it down. Then stick your thermometer a little way into a snowbank. Wait a few minutes before you pull it out and read it. Take the temperature of the snowbank in the middle and at the ground. Compare the readings that you wrote down. Is it warmer the deeper you go? Is the snowbank warmer than the air above?

That fluffy white blanket which seems so cold when you scoop it up to make snowballs really is a blanket after all.

You can measure the amount of air in snow. Scoop up some snow in a large can but do not pack it down. Take the can into your house and set it aside until the snow has melted. The amount of water you end up with, compared with the amount of snow you started with, will tell you what part of the snow was water and what part was air.

You should remember that the amount of air will not always be the same because the ice crystals that make up different snowstorms are not the same size and shape. Some crystals pack together more closely than others.

Would you like to measure a snowfall? Put a large tin can in a spot away from the house but not under a tree. The best place is on a bench or box above the ground. After a snowstorm take out a ruler and measure how much snow has fallen into the can. It is more fun if some of your friends do this too, so you can compare notes. On a calendar keep a record of the time and date when each snowstorm begins and ends and how many inches of snow fall. Keep your calendar so you can see how the weather next year compares with this year's.
SARA B. MURPHEY

35

In Northern Siberia there is a huge, treeless plain called the tundra that stretches for thousands of miles along the Arctic Ocean. This cold, cold land is almost completely flat, and the ground there is frozen straight down for hundreds of feet. The soil never thaws except for about three feet at the top, which thaw during the short summer and then freeze again in winter. During the summer, this thawed soil turns into swamps that stretch as far as one can see. Only patches of grass and a few bushes here and there grow in this vast land. Winters are even colder on the tundra than at the North Pole so few species of animals live there.

Only a few thousand years ago, millions of animals were living on the tundra. When some of these animals died, their bodies were quickly frozen solid and preserved. Today people are uncovering the remains of these creatures in many parts of Siberia and Alaska. If you were in the tundra walking along the frozen ground, you might be surprised by something sticking out of the ice that looked like an elephant's tusk. Equipped with a shovel, a pickax, and plenty of time, you might dig around your discovery and find the body of an ancient hairy elephant called a mammoth.

When you put a chicken in the freezer, you know that it will still taste good two or three months later. But did you know that frozen meat can keep for thousands and thousands of years?

Scientists think that mammoths lived about 10,000 years ago, and yet today, when people find their frozen bodies in the tundra, the meat is sometimes good enough to eat. In fact, mammoth steaks were once served at a banquet for Russian scientists.

There are other animals besides mammoths in the frozen tundra: rhinoceroses, saber-toothed cats, buffaloes, and many kinds of smaller animals. There are also millions of trees. One explorer found a 90-foot-tall fruit tree that had been blown down, covered with mud, and frozen. It still had leaves and ripe fruit on its branches!

For every complete body found in Siberia and Alaska there are also thousands of bones of animals that weren't so well preserved. Some islands in the Arctic Ocean seem to be composed almost entirely of bones. And many more bones are scattered over the bottom of the sea. Storms sometimes throw them onto the Arctic beaches.

How did all these animals manage to live on the tundra? Where did they find their food? How could they live through the winter? How were they caught and frozen before their flesh had time to spoil? Scientists don't know the answers to these questions for sure. Some of them think the mammoths died when they fell into icy lakes. Others believe that landslides might have buried many mammoths. But the whole story of these hairy elephants is still a mystery.
CHARLES HAPGOOD

In 1900, a dog led some Siberian hunters to the complete remains of an ancient mammoth.

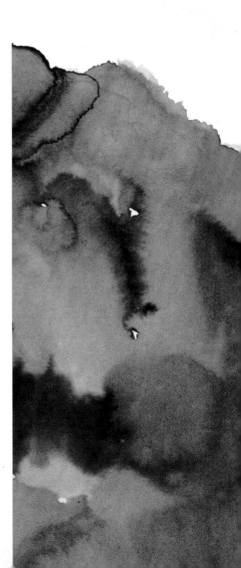

Monsters in the Ice

When Winter Comes

When winter comes, animals survive the bitter cold and lack of food in a variety of ways. Some head south to warmer climates. Others go underground or underwater to sleep until spring. Many more face the cold and stay active year-round.

Some of these active creatures, such as trout, pike and other cold-water fish, can go through winter with little change in their lifestyles. But before the first breath of frigid air, most other active animals must prepare for the cold. Deer, grouse and other warm-blooded animals build up layers of fat on their bodies for extra energy. Squirrels store nuts. Beavers stick twigs and branches into the mud at the bottom of their ponds. These will provide snacks all through the winter. Pikas, small mammals of the western mountains, store piles of dried grass for food.

Other animals must change their diets. Bluebirds give up their insect diet and eat mostly berries. Cottontail rabbits nibble twigs instead of juicy leaves.

Many mammals grow a heavier coat of fur which protects them from the cold. Deer grow extra hollow hairs which do a great job of keeping them warm. Musk oxen (1) grow a long, shaggy coat of hair over their soft under-coat. The long hair protects them from rain and snow, and the undercoat helps to hold in their body heat.

Birds keep in their body heat by fluffing out their feathers to make a thicker coat (2). Ducks and geese have undercoats of soft down to keep them warm. And bob-white quail snuggle together in a tight, cozy circle when they sleep at night.

Many other animals go into a deeper, winter-long sleep called hibernation to survive the cold.

Mammals such as ground-hogs and bats hibernate in burrows or caves where the air is warmer than outside. The body temperature of a

2

1

hibernating animal drops almost to freezing. Its breathing and heartbeat slow down. It is nourished by the fat it has stored in its body. Only one species of bird hibernates. It is the poorwill, a small gray brown bird found in the western United States.

Many people think that bears hibernate; but their body temperature stays almost normal and they can be wakened easily. They are just asleep, not hibernating. The bear's cubs are born during this long winter sleep.

Many kinds of ladybird beetles (also called ladybugs) (3) gather in huge clumps in sheltered places to hibernate. Most adult insects, such as

moths, grasshoppers and praying mantises, die before winter arrives. But they leave behind hibernating offspring —eggs, nymphs, larvae or pupae. And certain kinds of bees leave behind very important adults, the queens, which will lay next year's eggs.

3

Almost all cold-blooded creatures hibernate. Frogs and many toads burrow into the mud. Some species of rattlesnakes (4) clump together in a big ball inside a den.

Sometimes the outer snakes freeze to death, but those inside the clump survive the cold. Most freshwater pond fish—eels and bass, for instance—hibernate.

Some animals survive winter by leaving the cold country —they migrate. Some make very short trips. Mountain quail (5) walk downhill in single file to warmer valleys where they spend the winter. Certain fish, such as bluefish, migrate short distances to warmer water.

4

40

6

Other animals migrate a few hundred kilometers at most. Caribou of the Arctic move south from the tundra to find food and shelter in the forests. Canada geese fly south until they find water that doesn't freeze over and fields that are not snow-covered all winter. Many bluebirds fly south until they find places where there is plenty of food. Elk and black-tailed deer migrate vertically. In late fall heavy snow covers their food supplies, and they move down from high mountain summer ranges to warmer winter pastures on lower ground.

Some animals migrate great distances. The Arctic tern flies 17,500 kilometers (11,000 miles) from the Arctic to the tip of South America. And monarch butterflies (6) fly hundreds of kilometers to winter in southern climates.

Winter means long months of hardship for many animals. But one day a warm breeze blows from the south. Soon streams run full with melting snow and ice. Trees burst into bloom. And then, suddenly it seems, spring arrives. Robins return and sing their cheery songs. Moths stir in their cocoons. Frogs crawl from the mud. Groundhogs poke their sleepy heads from their burrows. Soon animal babies will be born. The wild creatures have survived another winter.
BOB GRAY

5

Tale of the Grouse

Snow fell all night long. A speckled brown bird the size of a small chicken was asleep in a tree. His feathers were fluffed out for warmth.

It was still snowing at dawn. The ruffed grouse cock shook the snow off and stretched each leg slowly. Balancing on his perch, he flapped his wings. Then he flew to a nearby apple orchard where he began searching in the soft snow for apples that had fallen from the trees.

During the night a deer had eaten most of the apples. There were only a few left for the grouse. But they were enough to fill his crop.

Meanwhile, a great horned owl patiently watched the busy grouse. It was waiting for the right moment to strike. Suddenly the crafty hunter left its perch.

Dropping quietly, the owl sank its sharp talons into the grouse's tail. The startled cock jumped and pulled free, leaving most of his tail feathers in the owl's iron grip. The grouse flew as fast as he could into the woods. The rest of the day he hid in a thick grove of spruce trees.

By dusk a very cold north wind began to blow. The snowstorm had become a

blizzard. Shivering in the wintry blast, the cock flew around looking for a snowdrift that would make a warm place to spend the night. He found one in the apple orchard.

Diving from a tall tree overlooking the orchard, the cock held his head back and struck the soft drift with his breast. The plunge carried him about 30 centimeters (1 foot) below the surface. Once underneath he pushed the powdery snow aside and made a small space for himself. He was as snug as an Eskimo in an igloo, and soon fell asleep. His snow cave held his body heat and insulated him from the cold.

That night the weather turned warmer. A mixture of rain and sleet fell. Frozen crystals began covering the soft snow. By early morning the temperature had dropped sharply, freezing the snow's wet surface into a thick, solid crust.

The grouse awoke and started to leave his insulated bed. He pushed upward, trying to break through the icy surface. Even though ruffed grouse are strong birds he couldn't get out. Rushing

about in panic, he formed a short tunnel in the snow. Soon he was so tired he collapsed. He was a prisoner under the snow. He would have no chance to escape if a predator were to discover him. How long would it take for the frozen crust to melt?

Before sunrise the next day a red fox padded cautiously across the slippery crust. A falling apple hit the crust directly above the grouse's tunnel, startling the fox. When the fox saw the apple he went after it. He tried to bite into it and accidentally pushed it away. Back and forth over the trapped grouse the fox stumbled, trying to get the fruit. The grouse held still with fright. The fox finally got a good hold on the apple and ate it quickly. He went away without hearing, seeing or smelling the grouse.

On the third day the sun was warmer and brighter. Wisps of fog floated low over the stream that ran through the orchard. A white-tailed doe nibbled lazily on the needles of a nearby spruce. Suddenly a blue jay whistled a warning call. The doe froze instantly. The scent of humans

reached her quivering nostrils. She raised her tail and ran into the woods.

A woman and her young daughter out for a hike came to the place where the deer had been standing. Looking at the tracks, the mother said, "Look, Meg, deer tracks. Let's walk back and see if it has a bed near here."

Crunching through the thick crust, Meg just missed stepping on the trapped grouse. With a clatter of strong, rapidly beating wings, the grouse burst out of the opening, showering Meg with loose snow. "What was that, Mom?" Meg asked, her eyes popping.

"Ruffed grouse," her mother answered, kicking the snow away to see where the bird had been. "I wonder how long that bird's been trapped here," she said. Then, after studying the hole for a moment, they went on.

Skimming low across a field, the grouse finally settled on a fallen log. Free at last, he sat preening himself. Before very long, spring would come. The snow would melt and the ruffed grouse would be ready for new adventures.

TOM MONSER

Naput and Nanook

Naput stopped. He felt a shiver of fright. There, not a hundred feet away, were three polar bears—a mother bear and two cubs.

In all of his years on earth, young Naput had never been so close to *Nanook*, the Big One. A few minutes before, he had left his father's hunting camp by himself. It was a bright, clear day and he felt like taking a hike. He had wandered out on the ocean ice pack, picking his way through jagged ice hummocks. Though he knew polar bears were around, Naput never even dreamed that he might run straight into a whole family of them. But—suddenly, there they were!

The bears were in a small ice valley. They had not seen Naput, and he quickly froze into a crouching statue. If the female saw him she would charge, thinking her cubs were in danger. And if she charged, it would very likely be the end of one small Eskimo boy.

Though frightened, Naput was also fascinated. The mother bear was very big. Naput judged her weight at nearly a thousand pounds. He had seen many bears while with his father, Nilliguk, and had learned to size them up. The cubs were small. They still had a lot of growing to do. Even so, they were already tall enough to look an arctic fox right in the eye.

The cubs played like puppies. They nipped at each other, and yipped in mock anger, but their mother ignored them. She was watching a seal hole in the ice. If a seal came up from the depths of the ocean for air, it might find itself becoming supper for Nanook. Polar bears eat more seal meat than any other kind.

A wind came up and rippled the fur on Naput's parka. The wind then swirled around the female bear and she growled. She swung her long neck around and stared directly at the boy. She had caught his scent in the wind! With a growl, she leaped forward and at the same time Naput leaped away.

How he ran! He ran as fast as the treacherous wind that had given him away. And as he ran, Naput yelled for help. "Father! Father!" Nilliguk had to be somewhere near. *Father!*

Glancing behind, the fleeing boy saw that Nanook was gaining fast. The bear was snarling horribly, her lips pulled back to show glistening ivory teeth. Naput had heard that polar bears grew forty-two teeth, and now he believed it! He had seen what those teeth did to seals, and he shuddered. There wasn't any doubt in his mind what would happen if the bear caught up with him. The boy's heart pounded in terror. His feet pounded even harder and he ran faster than he had ever run in his life.

What was it Nilliguk had said? "If you are chased by the ice bear, throw down some clothing. Nanook will stop to smell it."

The boy peeled off one of his mittens of denim and wool. He threw it down and ran a short distance. He chanced another look behind and found Nanook had stopped at the mitten. She had planted a huge front paw on it and was tearing it to shreds.

There was a chance. "Father!" he cried. "Father, help!" As if in answer to his cries, a rifle shot boomed in the arctic air. Then there was another!

A moment later, Nilliguk raced into view carrying the gun.

Naput ran into his father's waiting arms. "Father!" he exclaimed, nearly out of breath, "The Big One is after me!"

"Not now," was the reply. "You are safe with me."

Naput turned in time to see the bear running off onto the ice crags.

"I heard your cries," said Nilliguk. "Cries such as you made meant only one thing—something was after you. I fired the rifle hoping the sound would frighten whatever it was." Nilliguk's lined face wrinkled in a smile. "It did," he said.

The two started toward camp, Naput clutching his father's hand tightly. "It was a close call, Father," he admitted in a voice still shivery. "I nearly wound up in Nanook's stomach with part of my mitten."

The two laughed and Naput felt good.

That night, snug in their tent, Nilliguk talked about the polar bear. "The Big One is afraid of nothing and will kill and eat anything from seals to musk oxen. It may even kill people when it is hungry or angry enough."

"Ugh!" said Naput.

"But the mother loves her cubs very much," added Nilliguk. "She will fight for them. She is very protective. At sea the cubs hang onto mama if they tire of swimming. Sometimes they even take mama's tail in their mouths and she tows them."

Naput laughed. The thought of a couple of small cubs gripping their mother's tail with their teeth was funny. "Their teeth would sting," he said.

"Perhaps, but the mother doesn't seem to mind," was the reply.

Nilliguk pumped the fuel tank on the kerosene stove that heated the tent. The flames grew hotter and brighter. He set a kettle of water on for tea.

"Nanook can swim far without tiring," Naput's father said. "I have seen the Big One miles from shore. It is as much at home in the water as on land."

Naput thought about this, then he said, "The cubs were cute. I would like to have one for a pet."

Nilliguk shook his head. "They are too independent to be good pets," he said. "Though a cub weighs only two pounds when it is born, it weighs four hundred times that in two or three years. Could you hold an eight-hundred-pound bear in your lap?"

Naput decided that, indeed, he couldn't.

"When Nanook is only two years old it leaves its mother for life," continued Nilliguk. "It would leave you too."

"And the father polar bear doesn't stay around after the young are born," Nilliguk went on. "The mother drives him away."

"Why does she do that?" asked Naput.

"Because the father might eat his young. He has been known to do it."

"Ugh!" muttered Naput for the second time. He was quiet a moment, then added, "Do you know something, father?"

"Some things I know," replied Nilliguk with a grin. "But not everything. What did you want to say?"

"I am glad you are not a polar bear."
ROBERT H. REDDING

Sammy Squirrel's

Winter Adventures

Want to go exploring through the white winter woods with me? You do? Well, bundle up! My fur keeps *me* snug, but let me give you a tip or two to keep *you* warm and dry. Know why? You'll have more fun.

You like the outdoors, I can see. And you look to me like pretty good listeners and lookers and sniffers. But I can show you some woodland ways I bet you've never before noticed—like how to tell where animals have been by their tracks in the snow and their marks on the trees. We can see how many plants we can name. That's a good game.

Have you ever seen a real crystal castle? No? I'll take you to one, and I'll show you how to make an ice palace all your own. All you need are some bowls and funnels, maybe some cartons and cubes. Lots of imagination, of course—and ice.

And when your fantastic building is done, there's *more* fun—learning XCS, Cross-Country Skiing, that is. Not *me*, naturally, but I'll show you exactly how you can make some tracks of your own in the snow. Hey! How about giving me a ride?

Let's go.

Warm Tips for Winter Trips

Are you planning to hike, cross-country ski or build ice sculptures this winter? If so, make sure you know how to keep warm and safe before heading outdoors. Here are a few cold weather tips that will help you warm up to winter. To remember them, just think of their funny names.

FAT AND FEATHERS. Have you ever noticed how much fatter birds look in winter? It's because they fluff up their feathers so little pockets of air form between them. This trapped air helps hold in their body heat. Birds' feathers do the same job as mammals' fur or insulation in a building.

To keep yourself warm, put on several layers of clothes. The more layers you wear, the warmer you'll be. Like feathers, the layers will trap pockets of air that keep your body warmth from escaping.

PUDDLES AND POCKETS. Don't get wet by splashing in puddles or sitting in the snow. If water fills the tiny air pockets in your clothing, it will force the air out and let your body heat escape.

When that happens, head indoors right away, towel off in a warm room and put on some dry clothes.

COCOA AND CAPS. If you blow on a hot cup of cocoa, the cocoa soon becomes cool enough to drink. Blowing removes the warm air above the hot liquid and cools it quickly.

Wind cools your warm body in the same way. Your body is always making and losing heat. Much of that heat is lost from your head and neck.

When the wind whisks away the warm air around your head, your body slows the blood supply to your feet and hands. This makes them feel cold. So wear a cap on cold, windy days and you'll keep your hands and feet warmer.

CANDY AND COOKING. Did you know that your body "cooks" with fuel almost as a stove cooks with gas or electricity? Your body's fuel is food and it produces heat and energy as it is "burned" inside you.

Candy is a quick-burning fuel. So eating it when you are cold will quickly furnish fuel for your body. What a great excuse to carry candy in your pocket when you're outdoors!

SHOVELING AND SHIVERING. When you use your muscles to skate or run, your body burns up its fuel. So the more active you are, the more fuel you'll burn, and the warmer you'll become.

Sometimes you haven't exercised enough to keep warm and your body will automatically exercise for you by shivering. When that happens, your muscles are working to make the heat you need to stay comfortable. Move around more and you'll stop shivering.

HUFFING AND HEATING. When you "huff" onto a mirror, the moisture in your warm breath forms a mist on the cold glass. Your skin gives off moisture too. And the warmer you get, the more moisture you give off. This is one of your body's ways of cooling itself. If you get too warm while outside, this moisture collects on the inside of your cool clothes and makes you cool. So unzip your jacket or peel off a layer of clothes to get comfortable again.
ROBERT H. MEIER

Walk in the Winter Woods

1

Whether balancing on a snowy log (1) or tramping across snowy trails, you'll have more fun if you wear waterproof boots to keep your feet warm and dry.

In spite of a heavy glaze of ice, mountain laurel (2) keeps its shiny, green leaves throughout the winter months.

2

Don't hole up and hibernate in winter as some animals do. Bundle up in your warmest clothes and go out into the woods. A walk in the winter woods can be fun.

If it is late winter and you think spring is never going to come, just look around you at the tips of branches. You will be surprised to see so much color. The red maple buds seem almost ready to burst and soon the sap will be rising in the sugar maples. In winter when many of the trees are bare, it's fun to see if you know which tree is which. Look closely and you will notice the differences in the buds. Then stand back and look at the shape of the tree and the color and pattern of the bark. If you examine the trees carefully enough, you'll soon be able to tell the different kinds apart.

Winter is a good time to learn about conifers too. These cone-bearing trees and shrubs drop their needles throughout the year. If you stand quietly in an evergreen forest, you will find this out. You may also notice that there are many different kinds of conifers. Some, such

Frost outlines nature's show of Christmas colors—green plants and a red maple leaf (3).

A holly's bright red berries (4) are good winter food for birds and its foliage gives them protection from bad weather and predators.

Plant buds can help you learn which tree or shrub is which in the winter landscape. Lilac (5), for example, has green or reddish buds surrounded by two or three thick scales.

You're more likely to see the fruits of English ivy (6), a common backyard vine, when it's growing in the wild.

as hemlock, have very short needles. Others have long needles, like the pines. Still others are in between, like spruce and fir.

One of the nicest sights is on the edge of the woods. In a snowstorm, dry, leftover flowers like goldenrod and Queen Anne's lace catch and hold the flakes in beautiful patterns. Ice storms, though sometimes damaging to trees, turn the woods into a glittering wonderland. Stems and branches sparkle in their coating of ice, and the grass and berries shimmer like Christmas ornaments.

The animals that live in the winter woods are often hard to find. But if you are a good detective, you will learn to read the signs they leave behind. Each of these messages tells a story. You can figure out whether a rabbit or a squirrel crossed your path by the tracks it left in the snow. Sometimes snow trails tell stories that have sudden endings. A tiny mouse trail may end in blood and fur with the wing marks of a hawk or owl nearby on the snow.

Did you ever look closely at chewed branches of shrubs and trees? The special tooth-marks that animals leave give them away. A bunny makes a clean cut while a deer has to tear twigs because it does not have any teeth in the front part of its upper jaw.

At the base of a large pine tree you may see big chips of wood lying on the snow. This is your signal to look up the trunk. You may see the holes made by a wood-pecker. When one of these birds goes after a grub buried in the trunk, it hammers out those wood chips with its strong beak.

Over in the shrubs is a huge ice cream cone! Last summer's bird's nest has caught the soft snow and held it—white against the black twigs. When we brush off the snow to peek, it looks like someone's leftover lunch inside. A mouse has moved in for the winter.

Farther along where some fruits have fallen from the berry bushes, the mice have paid a visit. Their dizzy tracks go in and out over the snow and finally end at a hole. The heat from their small bodies has frosted the edge of the hole, trimming it in icy lace.

Chickadees hop from branch to branch among the birches, knocking down a shower of seeds. Soon other woodland animals will come along and make a midwinter feast of the tiny seeds.

If you are lucky you may find an empty hornets' nest swinging from a tree limb. You can examine it and see that these insects have really found the answer to insulation. Count the thin papery layers with air space between that cover the inner cells. Have you ever watched a football game outdoors when it was very cold and put newspaper under your feet to keep warm? If you have, then you realize that hornets have known this trick for a long time.

One of the best finds of all is a dry, brown, baglike object about an inch and a half to two inches long hanging from a branch. Collect this egg case and keep it outdoors until spring. Then watch it carefully. One warm day, more than 200 tiny praying mantises will hatch from it.

By now your feet and hands are probably getting cold. It's time to go indoors for hot cocoa and popcorn.
RUTH SMILEY

The evening grosbeak (9) lives mostly on seeds during cold weather. When you walk in the woods, you may see these birds pecking at locust and ash seeds. But at the feeder, sunflower seeds are their favorite.

The morning after an ice storm, a fox squirrel (10) comes out to find something to eat. Fox squirrels gather nuts in the fall and bury each one separately. When winter comes, they head back to the area where their supplies are hidden and sniff around to find the nuts again.

Snowshoe hares (7) have white coats in winter so predators will have a hard time spotting them in the snow.

You probably won't see a beaver in the winter woods. But if you're near water, you may notice signs of its presence—lodges, dams, gnawed trees, and trees stripped of bark (8).

55

Who Went There?

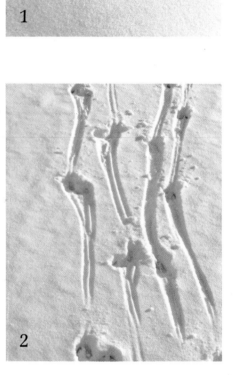

A red fox creeps silently through the woods. You might never know who had been there if you couldn't read its message "foot"-printed in snow.

Following animals' tracks is one of the best ways to study their habits. The marks can tell you whether a creature was running, walking, going in a definite direction, or just out for a stroll.

Can you figure out what animals made the tracks in each photo? If you need help, match the word clues to the photos. Then write the photo numbers in the boxes.

56

4

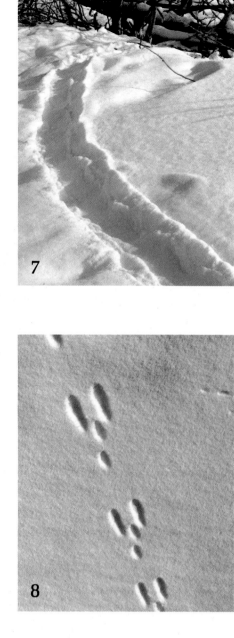

7

5

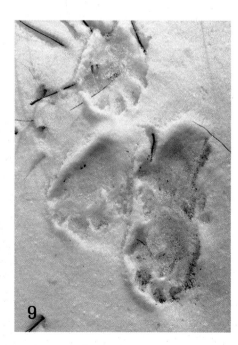

8

6

9

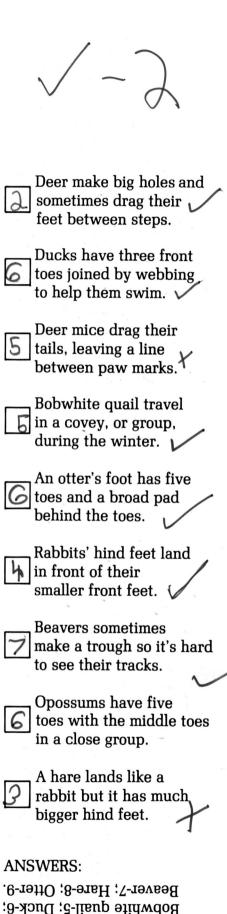

2 Deer make big holes and sometimes drag their feet between steps. ✓

6 Ducks have three front toes joined by webbing to help them swim. ✓

5 Deer mice drag their tails, leaving a line between paw marks. ✗

5 Bobwhite quail travel in a covey, or group, during the winter. ✓

6 An otter's foot has five toes and a broad pad behind the toes. ✓

4 Rabbits' hind feet land in front of their smaller front feet. ✓

7 Beavers sometimes make a trough so it's hard to see their tracks. ✓

6 Opossums have five toes with the middle toes in a close group.

3 A hare lands like a rabbit but it has much bigger hind feet. ✗

ANSWERS:
Deer mouse-1;
Deer-2; Opossum-3; Rabbit-4;
Bobwhite quail-5; Duck-6;
Beaver-7; Hare-8; Otter-9.

57

Crystal Castle

The frigid winter months are the perfect time to build a glittering ice castle. And if the cold lasts, your crystal creation will stand for days.

All you need are kitchen and grocery containers for molds and some water. Your molds must be plastic, rubber or metal—*not glass*. When water freezes, it expands and breaks a glass container. You should also pick molds that are straight-sided or larger at the top than at the bottom so the ice can be removed.

To get you started, here's a sampling of castle parts and molds that you can use to duplicate them.

Stacked plastic bowls with water in both bowls make solid domes and thin bowl-domes.

Plastic lids make thin discs.

Various food molds make a variety of patterned shapes.

Ice cube trays make bricks for walls and foundations.

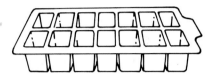

Fancy new ice cube trays make tiny knobs.

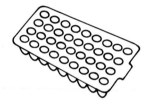

Basters with the rubber ball removed and the small end plugged make tall spires.

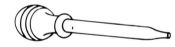

Clear plastic toy packaging makes mysterious shapes that will look almost familiar.

Plastic soda straws make bridges between towers.

Plastic Easter egg halves or styrene egg cartons make small half-domes.

Funnels with the small ends plugged (gum makes a good plug) make cones with spires.

Plastic meat trays from the grocery store make fancy walls and roofs of patterned sheets of ice.

Cupcake pans make very thick discs.

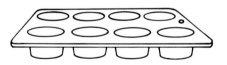

Cookie molds make decorations for walls and towers.

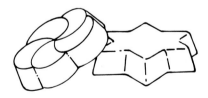

WARNING
Do not handle freezing-cold metal molds without gloves or plastic bags over your hands. The metal will freeze to your skin and hurt you.

On a freezing day, take your molds outside and fill them with water. Add a few drops of food coloring to the water if you'd like your castle to be colorful. Then leave the molds outdoors until the water freezes solid.

The construction site for your castle should be in partial shade. That way it won't melt too quickly and a little

sunlight will highlight the palace with sparkles.

When you're ready to begin building, check the air temperature to make sure it's freezing (0° C) or below. Then dip the molds into a bucket of warm water for a few seconds until the ice shapes slide out easily. Use a spray-bottle of water to freeze-weld the ice pieces together. A little snow

is a big help in holding your first ice walls in position. But if there is no snow, spray the ground and the edges to be joined, and hold the pieces in place until they freeze together.

As a final touch for your castle, go icicle hunting for some tall spires and add a few colored marbles.
CHARLEEN KINSER

59

Skiing Through Winter

Kick-glide-kick-glide. The easy rhythm of cross-country skiing carries you along the trail. Only animal tracks break the fresh snow that lies ahead. You've entered a magical white world—you've skied into winter.

Cross-country skiing, X C S for short, has been around for a long time. Centuries ago Norsemen skied with boards tied to their feet to keep from sinking in deep snow.

Then people in the Swiss Alps discovered how much fun it was to zoom down mountainsides. That was the start of another very popular sport, downhill skiing. But downhill slopes have become so crowded in recent years that many families are heading out on cross-country skis again.

One such family is the Davenports from Woodstock, Vermont. Last year Karen, 9, Jim, 6, and their parents gave each other X C S outfits for Christmas. Polly, 2, enjoys family ski trips from a rucksack on her father's back.

Charley, an Eskimo friend from Alaska, often joins the Davenport trips. His grandfather, a hunter, made Charley's first skis from barrel staves and sealskin. The skins line the bottom of the skis so a skier can go uphill without sliding backwards. With regular X C skis special waxes serve the same purpose.

On a typical day trip, the Davenports start with two hours of gentle up- and downhill traveling across the countryside. Jim leads the group,

breaking a path through the fresh snow. Soon the family feels completely alone in an untracked world of white. But they're not really alone. Animal tracks crisscross the snow. They help Karen spot a rabbit disappearing into the tall bushes.

By noon everyone is warm from the exercise and hungry for the lunch they've brought along. The group finds a hilltop site with a beautiful view and makes a lunch stop.

The afternoon trip is a little harder; there are many steep hills to conquer. It's the downhill slopes that get really tricky. The soft X C S boots that are so comfortable going uphill and on flat surfaces, give little support for downhill control.

Slowing down is another problem. The Davenports drag ski poles alongside, pushing down on them to slow their descent. If this doesn't work, they just sit down in the snow.

Besides carrying you into a spectacular white world, your X C S equipment has other advantages. It costs less than downhill equipment. It's also lighter and easier to handle and can be used by people of all ages.

The snow is there. The countryside is there. Ask your family to give X C S a try.
HANSON CARROLL

1

X C S bindings (1) can be two cables or a clamp that holds the toe of a flexible boot to the ski.

With the heel free, a X C skier makes a smooth, jogging-like step to cross the snow.

Ah, at last it's lunchtime (2). After a couple of hours of energetic X C S, everyone has worked up a huge appetite.

Jim takes the lead (3), breaking a trail through the deep snow for the rest of the group.

Jim uses a skating motion and thrusts of his poles to ski over deep snow (4). The length and width of X C skis spread his weight so he doesn't sink.

Ollie Otter's

Fun Pages

Like to make things? Me too! In nothing flat I can turn a hillside into a mudslide, a snowbank into a chute! I don't know why, but I like best the things *I* make. You too?

Then come on, let me show you how, in Mexico, people take a little bit of yarn, twist it this way and that—and presto, an animal or a flower for decoration. Then we'll see how, in Scandinavia, folks make wonderful wood shapes, and in Poland, how they make stars to hang on the Christmas tree.

Holidays! They mean brightness and color and fun, don't they! Well, I know three kinds of lights you can make—candles, can-delabra, and luminarios. I'll explain. And have you ever made fancy animal cookies—to munch or to hang on a tree? Watch me!

On Christmas Eve, while you're waiting to hear reindeer hoofs on your roof, you can easily make (and play with) your own reindeer puppets! I'll show you how.

And for wrappings, guess what! You can design your very own holiday cheer! *That* makes a gift just about as special as it can be, seems to me.

Let's start merry making!

Ornaments From Many Lands

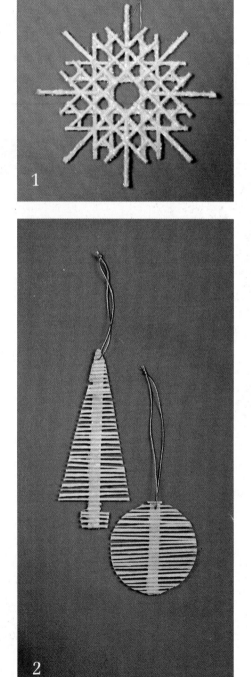

The look of Christmas is a little different everywhere you go. That's because each country has its own special holiday customs. In Scandinavia, Christmas trees may be dotted with wood ornaments, while snowflakes decorate German trees. This year, start a new tradition in your house—an international tree with ornaments you've made.

1 GERMAN SNOWFLAKES
Cut a snowflake shape from the bottom of a berry basket (the plastic container in which berries are sold). Cut a different snowflake shape from another berry basket. Glue the two shapes together. Paint. Before the paint dries, sprinkle with diamond dust or glitter that you've bought in a hobby store.

2 SCANDINAVIAN ORNAMENTS
Center and then glue flat wood toothpicks to a paste or Popsicle stick. Let the glue dry completely. In pencil, draw the outline of a bell, tree, Christmas ball, or any other shape you like on the toothpicks. Then cut along the pencil line. Poke a small hole at the top of your ornament for a hanger.

3 UKRAINIAN COBWEBS
Draw a cobweb on a piece of paper. Cover the paper with plastic wrap. Squeeze white glue along the outline of the web and press string into the glue. Let the glue dry and then gently lift the cobweb from the plastic wrap. Paint the web with a thin coat of glue and sprinkle it with diamond dust.

4 MEXICAN YARN ANIMALS
Draw an animal or plant design on a piece of heavy cardboard. Cut around the outline of your drawing. Squeeze white glue along the lines of the design and press brightly colored pieces of yarn into the glue. Spread more glue on the rest of the cardboard shape and press other colors of yarn into the glue.

5 POLISH STARS
Glue three toothpicks together to form a triangle. Make another triangle. Glue the two triangles together to form a star. Paint. To make pom-poms, wrap yarn around your closed fingers ten times. Remove and tie the bundle in the center to form a figure 8. Cut the loops and fluff the ends of the yarn. Glue a pom-pom to each point of the star.

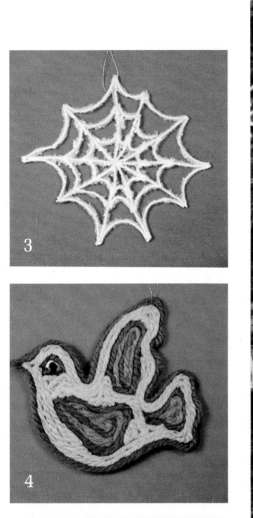

3

4

5

Light Up Your Holidays

On a dark night in December, what could be prettier than bright, colorful candles and candleholders? And what would be even better than using ones you have made?

TIN CAN-DELABRA

Tin candleholders add a lot of sparkle to a holiday table. You can make your own with a tin can, a hammer, a nail and a piece of wood.

First wash and dry your tin can. Make sure the top is smooth. Rough edges can cut.

Draw your design on a piece of paper. Tape the design onto the can. At right we've used designs of a snowflake and lighted candles.

Find a piece of wood about the same size as the can. Place this inside the can to help it keep its shape when you hammer. Now, using a hammer and nail, outline your design with nail holes.

LUMINARIOS

Set up along a sidewalk or a driveway, luminarios (paper bags with candles inside) make beautiful *outdoor* decorations. Start with paper bags, foil, glue, small candles, and sand.

To make your luminario, fold the top of an open paper bag over and over until it's three or four inches shorter. Cut shapes out of foil and glue them to the bag for decorations.

Fill the bag at least one-third full with sand. Stick a candle in the sand and make sure it doesn't wobble. If it does, add more sand. Get a grown-up to help you light the candle inside the bag.

ICEBERG CANDLES

These ice-blue candles marked with strange holes remind some people of icebergs. All you need are a plain candle, ice cubes, paraffin, a blue crayon, and a milk carton.

First, trim the carton to the height you want. Cut down a plain candle to the same height and hold it in the center of the carton. Drop ice cubes around the candle until you have filled the carton. Put it in the sink.

Next, melt paraffin over boiling water in the top of a double boiler. (Never heat paraffin in a regular pot. It may catch fire.) *Get a grown-up to help you with this step.* Add a piece of blue crayon for color.

When the paraffin is melted, pour it into your ice-filled mold. Then when it hardens, tear away the carton and shake out the water.

Tasty Trimmings

Here's a holiday craft that you can hang on your tree, give to your friends, or eat all by yourself. You'll find these tasty trimmings lots of fun to bake because you must become both an artist and a chef. And the spicy smell of gingerbread will make the cookies a favorite holiday tradition for your entire family.

Before you begin, make sure that an adult will be nearby when you use the stove. Then gather all the ingredients listed in the recipes on the right and follow the step-by-step instructions.

GINGERBREAD COOKIES

5-1/2 cups flour
3 teaspoons baking soda
1-3/4 cups dark brown
    sugar, firmly packed
1/4 cup dark molasses
4-1/2 teaspoons ground
    cinnamon
3 teaspoons ground ginger
1/2 teaspoon ground
    cloves
1/4 teaspoon salt
1/2 pound butter or
    margarine, melted
1/2 cup water, boiling
1 egg, beaten

ICING

1 cup confectioner's
    sugar, sifted
1 to 2 tablespoons milk
1/4 teaspoon vanilla
Food coloring
Shredded coconut
Colored sprinkles

This cookie craft can be fun to try by yourself or with a friend. Ronnit Bendavid-Val and Robert Davenport, our chefs, said they liked working together to make the dough. But each one formed and decorated different "wild" cookies to hang on a tree.

STEP 1: Gather all the ingredients for the cookies. Then combine the flour and baking soda in a big bowl. Put this mixture aside until you need it in Step 4.

STEP 2: Now it's time to mix the spicy ingredients. Take out another large bowl and in it combine the brown sugar, dark molasses, ground cinnamon, ground ginger, ground cloves, and salt. Stir the mixture a few times with a large spoon.

STEP 3: Now melt the butter and heat the water until it boils. Add your hot butter and water to the brown sugar mixture and beat the batter until the sugar dissolves and the batter becomes smooth. That should take about three or four minutes.

STEP 4: Bit by bit, stir the flour mixture into your batter until it forms a stiff dough. This mixture will keep in your refrigerator for a couple of days if you want to make it ahead of time. But let the dough reach room temperature before making the cookies.

STEP 5: Now, on a greased cookie sheet, shape your cookies into animals (above). Make sure they aren't over 3/4'' thick at the highest point or they will lose their shape.

STEP 6: Brush the cookies with beaten egg and bake them in a 300° oven for 20 to 30 minutes. They're done when golden around the edges. Cool for 10 minutes.

STEP 7: Mix the icing and spoon some into separate bowls for each color. Add food coloring. Paint and decorate with sprinkles or coconut before the icing dries (below).

Reindeer Puppets

When you think of Christmas, do you usually think of Santa Claus, the North Pole, and reindeer? Lots of kids do. So what could be a more perfect gift for your friends than a family of reindeer puppets?

For each reindeer, you'll need: 16 strips of black paper, ½ inch wide; brown paint;

glue; string, 36" long; two toilet paper tubes; scraps of paper; and scissors.

1. To make the reindeer's legs, join two strips of paper as shown. Fold strip A over strip B, and then B over A.

Continue folding one strip over the other until both have been used up. Make 8 paper springs. Glue two springs end to end for each leg.

2. Make a slanted cut near the end of one of the tubes for the reindeer's head. Then glue paper over the ends of each tube. Glue the two tubes together to make the reindeer's body and head.

3. Paint the reindeer brown.

4. Cut out ears, antlers, eyes, a nose, a mouth, and a tail and glue them on.

Glue on the spring legs and attach one end of a 36" string to the reindeer's head and the other end to its body.

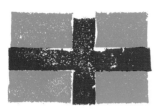

Stamp-Out Wrappings

Rubber stamps are fun to make and even more fun to use! At holiday time, you can design your own stamp-out wrappings so your friends' presents will look very special. You can also turn your stamp-out art into gifts. Try making stationery, envelopes, greeting cards, and bookmarks decorated with your art. You might even want to stamp your designs onto plain T-shirts. Your friends and family will love all of these gifts—because they're useful and they're specially designed by you.

To show you how to make a rubber stamp, Eddie Zarecour and Tracy Hamilton worked on some holiday stamps for wrapping paper. Follow each step carefully, always pointing the knife blade away from you when you're carving, and you're going to have lots of fun!

> **YOU WILL NEED**
> Pocket knife or a kitchen knife
> Art gum or soap erasers
> Stamp pads or poster paints and brush (If you're stamping on fabric, use acrylic paints or fabric inks, available in art and hobby stores.)

STEP 1: Draw your design on an eraser. Simple shapes are easiest to cut out and print the best. For a few stamp ideas, look at the designs above. Some are made from two separate stamps, each inked with a different color.

Now take out your knife and cut carefully along the outline of your design. You don't have to cut very deep—about 1/16". Then cut away a 1/16" layer of the area around your design. You should cut from the edge of the eraser to the outline of your design. Be careful and remember to cut away from yourself.

STEP 2: Next, put ink on your stamp. You can buy ink pads which come in many colors. Or you can color your stamp with a brush and paint. Now you're ready to stamp out your wrappings. Put several layers of newspaper under whatever you are stamping. This helps give a clearer print.

STEP 3: Now you're ready to start wrapping.

STEP 4: Eddie and Tracy like the last step in creating their stamp-out wrappings too—exchanging gifts.

Ranger Rick's

Christmas Eve Stories

Every Christmas Eve I'm chock full of big wishes! Aren't you? Don't you fall asleep hoping tomorrow will bring peace and joy to the world, to your friends—and a special present or two for you?

In Deep Green Wood Christmas always means thanks for a whole year of friendship and adventure, plenty of hard work and lots of good fun. And *my* Christmas Eve wish is for more of the same next year and every year to come.

There are several great stories about Christmas Eve wishes. Here are a couple of my favorites. One's about a sweet little old lady named Lolly and her spider friends. Lolly wishes she had a gaily decorated Christmas tree, but she's too poor to buy pretty things. Another story's about a small, young fir tree that wishes it could be brightly trimmed, important and useful. But it's too scraggly to be a fine Christmas tree. Nobody wants it.

Sometimes Christmas Eve wishes come true and sometimes they don't. Half the fun's in the dreaming, though, isn't it!—and half in Christmas surprises!

Happy Christmas to you!

The Little Old Lady Who Liked Spiders

O nce there was a little old lady named Lolly who liked spiders. There were spider webs in every nook and cranny and corner of her house in every size, shape, and design you could imagine. Some of the spiders were funnel weavers, some were orb weavers, and some were cobweb weavers. And there were also the wolf spiders and jumping spiders that didn't spin any webs at all, but could run with surprising speed along the floors, up the walls, and even upside down over the ceilings.

When the little old lady cleaned house— which, truth to tell, wasn't all that often—she would very carefully look over each spider web just to make sure it was old and abandoned before she swept it up. If a spider was at home, the little old lady would wish her a good morning and clean off the spider's front stoop for her.

All through the summer, Lolly watched the mother spiders carefully guarding their egg sacs. And when the spiderlings hatched out, she saw swarms of baby spiders spreading out along their mothers' web lines. Then she watched the babies going off to their own corners to spin their own little webs—all exactly like their mothers', but smaller.

Now Christmas was coming and Lolly thought about putting up a Christmas tree. She rummaged around in the attic until, at last, under a big box of Valentines, she found the Christmas ornaments. Because she didn't have much money, Lolly used the same decorations over and over again, year after year.

This year they looked thinner and more bedraggled than ever before. The star had lost its twinkle and the balls their glitter long ago. Empty loops of wire—all that was left of wings —dangled from the angels' backs, and the leaves and berries of the holly wreath were bent and broken.

On Christmas Eve Lolly went out to buy a small tree, but by that time, nearly all the good ones had been taken. She finally found one, brought it home, and stood it on a table in a corner of the living room. And then even Lolly could see it was a sad looking tree. She sighed a very deep sigh, and all the spider webs in the living room vibrated softly with her.

She fastened the wreath on the door, hung the few ornaments on the tree, and stepped back to look at the result. It wasn't much. The living room seemed melancholy and depressing in spite of the tree.

Lolly made some hot tea and sat for a moment holding it, warming her hands. Then she smiled and lifted her cup to toast the tree and the night. In a little while, she turned out the lights and slowly climbed the stairs to her bedroom, her carpet slippers softly slap-slapping as she went from step to step.

Well, you know that every Christmas Eve a very fantastic and wonderful thing happens. On that one night of the year, all the animals are able to talk, and, of course, spiders are no exception. At the stroke of midnight, they become regular chatterboxes.

The wolf spiders and the jumping spiders were the first to notice the sad little tree with its thread-bare decorations. Because these spiders stalk and catch their prey much as cats do, they have very keen eyes and little escapes their attention.

The news, however, had to be carried to the web weavers. They have rather poor eyesight and must depend on vibrations of their webs to find out what's what.

The spiders all liked the little old lady, because she was so very careful not to step on them or sweep them up. They thought and thought about what they might do to make this Christmas happy for her. Some said, "Why don't we give her a fly or two all wrapped up in spider silk?" This was the nicest thing they could think of. Flies were hard to get in

the middle of winter, and the gift would be a real sacrifice for them. But others said, "No, we don't think that would be a good present because we've never seen her eat flies."

So they thought and thought and thought some more. What else did they have that Lolly might like? Then one jumping spider, whose name was Victoria, had an idea.

"Tell the funnel weavers, the orb weavers, and the cobweb weavers to come to the Christmas tree," she said to the other wolf spiders and jumping spiders.

They rushed to carry out Victoria's orders, and such a scurrying has seldom been seen as all the spiders gathered under the tree.

Victoria, who had eight marvelous black eyes and lovely white spots on her black furry back, took charge of the operation. Her bright green jaws seemed to glitter as she outlined her plan. And you could see that with her regal bearing she made a very good chief engineer.

She directed all the funnel weavers, the orb weavers, and the cobweb weavers to spread out over the Christmas tree and to start weaving their webs. The jumping spiders and the wolf spiders were to be the leaders.

If you could have listened very, very closely (for, after all, spiders don't have particularly

loud voices) you might have heard, "That's very good, Josephine, but spread it out a little more, can't you? Try to move that top strand closer to Harriet's, there on your right."

"No, no, Helen, you're too far over into Janet's area. Climb a little bit higher to that empty space just under the star."

"Beautiful, beautiful, Eloise. That certainly does look lovely. It's exactly right."

Throughout the entire operation, Victoria was everywhere. She surveyed all the branches on the tree so she could tell where to place webs for the best effect. She examined the ornaments to see what might be done to refurbish them. Finally, she tested lines for tautness and strength and inspected finished webs for design and spacing.

At last the tree was completely covered with silvery strands of spider webs that shone and shimmered softly in the moonlight. Every ornament was encased in a dainty, elegant web, or wrapped in fine spider silk that took on the color of the ornament: red, blue, green, silver, or gold. The angels had new wings of gossamer, and the star at the top of the tree twinkled again.

The spiders had never seen anything more beautiful. As they climbed down the tree, they admired each other's work. They even had a compliment or two for the cobweb weavers; after all, it was now Christmas morning.

The sun shining into the window made the Christmas tree glow as red as fire. The spiders had returned to their home webs by this time— exhausted but happy.

Soon they heard the thump, thump of slippered feet. It was Lolly trudging down the stairs. She stumped toward the kitchen, for she was never fully awake in the morning until she had a cup or two of coffee.

But today something startled her awake. She wheeled around and rubbed her eyes. She looked and rubbed them again. She could not believe what she saw. That couldn't be *her* Christmas tree! Not the little one she had put up only last night. This tree was beautiful; it gleamed in the morning sunlight.

Lolly came closer and saw that the shining tree was covered with exquisite spider webs, woven in the most intricate designs. The spiders really had outdone themselves. There were cones and stars, circles and spirals, cones within cones, stars within stars, circles within circles, spirals within spirals. Spirals and cones were inside circles and stars; and snowflakes were everywhere.

Even the disorganized webs of the cobweb weavers, instead of distracting from the design, served as a kind of netting to bind the whole thing together.

Lolly laughed; she laughed so hard that tears streamed down her cheeks. She turned and smiled at all the corners and the doorways and the windows and at all the spider webs in their nooks and crannies that were now vibrating with happiness. Wiping her cheeks, she said, "Thank you, my friends, for the loveliest Christmas present I ever had."

And at the very top of the tree, sitting on the star in the radiance of the sun, Victoria nodded graciously.
EILEEN SNYDER

The Sea Christmas

It was a gray November day when the Cady family—Jane, her little brother Toppy, and their mother and father—moved back to Kettle Neck. Mr. Cady had been too ill to work lately, so they were saving money by giving up their city apartment and returning to a summer cottage they owned on the south shore of Long Island.

Jonas, the spaniel, was wild with excitement as country smells came into the car. He ploughed over people's feet and clawed at their knees trying to look out the window.

Toppy was nearly as bad. He bounced and jarred everyone and shouted, "Oh, man! Oh, brother! Kettle Neck all winter!"

Their street, Sea Street, was really only a road. On one side of it lay the big potato fields, deep emerald in the twilight, planted now in cover crops of rye and winter wheat that would hold the earth in place under the great winds of winter. On the other side a row of summer cottages stood boarded up, lonely among their shivering trees.

The Cadys' little house when they turned in the drive was as dark as all the other summer cottages. Cold salt wind struck their faces, and there was a loud, stormy roaring from the sea. When Mr. and Mrs. Cady fearfully unlocked the front door, warmth came towards them. A fire burned, safely screened in the fireplace; and when they snapped on the lights they found a note on the mantel:

"Welcome back, Mr. and Mrs. Cady and kids. Wood in garage. Food in icebox. Gas in tank. Yours truly, Elbert M. Hatchwood."

To the children the return to the cottage seemed like the best thing that had ever happened to them. At bedtime, when Jane put out her light and opened her window, the sea wind whistled in, smelling of herring. She could hear the surf, and nearer at hand in the dead garden, the rattling of dry corn leaves against the stalks.

As things turned out, it was only Toppy who could go to school in the small community. There was room for him in his class at the district school, but there was none for Jane in hers. "At least until after the Christmas holidays," the school principal had to tell them regretfully.

With Toppy in school, Jane was often alone, but she was never lonely. She loved the novelty of being at Kettle Neck in wintertime. With its bare trees and green, empty fields it seemed a very different place from what they had known in summer.

Whenever Jane went down to the water's edge, she and Jonas had the beach all to themselves. The only people they ever saw were the fishermen who came down early on calm days, putting out in rowboats to set their seines, reeling them in later on winches.

Often sandpipers shimmered along at the foam's edge, and Jane would follow the high-tide mark, bent over, examining, like a ragpicker looking for valuables. Many times she found them.

Every day the sea-litter was different. Sometimes there would be hundreds of tiny pink shells, like anemone petals, scattered among the weed and pebbles. Sometimes there was an abundance of mussel-wings, neatly paired and blue as jay feathers.

But the best thing to find was the seaglass. She had never paid much attention to it in the summertime, but now she searched, as if she were searching for jewels, for those bits of broken jar and bottle that had been rubbed in the sand and turned over and over by the tides. Scoured and scrubbed and worn for years, they were as smooth as pebbles, but were of far more lovely colors: sapphire, emerald, amethyst.

The days were mild for the time of year; many of them were fair. At night the skies were huge and different. Jane always enjoyed looking up while Jonas had his final run; sometimes a moon raced in the clouds, and sometimes there were only stars. Once there were northern lights. They woke Toppy up for

those and he came out, half asleep, wrapped to the ears in a big striped blanket. Great canopies were being draped and rearranged all over the sky; vast flutings of pearly white and green, faint stains of rose.

Thanksgiving came and went; soon it would be Christmas time. Jane worried about that. She had no presents to give to anyone and not a penny to buy them with.

What am I going to do, she wondered. I could write a poem for everyone, but that isn't really a present, and Toppy would be disgusted. She was very worried.

One day, a slow, cold, gray day, she went to the beach, carrying a basket her mother had given her for holding her sea treasures.

The sea rolled its waves, well spaced and somber, on the shore. Everything it had brought up was large—large straps of kelp, large ocean clam shells, large stones—nothing for the basket.

It was not long before she saw something rolling in the foam, rolling forward, then back—a round, green bobbing thing. Jane knew what it was at once; hurriedly she pulled off her shoes and socks, rolled up her jeans, and ran into the icy foam. It was a glass marker-buoy from a seine, a green glass ball closed in a net and stuck with barnacles and tiny mussels: something she had wanted to find for years!

Toppy had wanted to find one, too. He was always searching for one.

"But it would look so nice in my room," Jane said to Jonas.

"And it's the first one I ever found," she added a few minutes later.

"Oh, all *right*," she said at last. "Toppy can have it. It will be his Christmas present."

The next thing she found was a large black feather with a white polka dot near the tip. Surely she could do something with that. And then she found another, and then a whole cluster. Some poor herring gull had come to grief, but Jane wouldn't worry about that now.

"I know! I'll make Toppy an Indian war bonnet!" she said. "A really good one that hangs down at the back, not the crumby little ten-cent-store kind."

That left her father and mother.

That afternoon, wandering among the dunes, she came upon a leafless bayberry bush. She noticed how each of its upthrust branches was like a little tree—a very old and complicated little tree with many twigs and branches—and all at once she knew what she would make for her mother's present!

"A glass tree!" she told Jonas exultantly. "It will be a sort of tiny Christmas tree, but hung with pieces of glass for ornaments."

She went home to get her mother's pruning shears, and when she had chosen and clipped the prettiest, fanciest little tree, she took it back and smuggled it up to her room.

Then began a time of toil and trial for Jane. The war bonnet was easy. Her mother found her a long strip of scarlet felt; and all Jane had to do was to cut a pair of slits to hold each quill, secure it with thread, and sew it at the back to make a headband.

But the glass tree was not easy. The first part was all right. She simply took an old sand pail, painted it green, and filled it with plasticene. She stuck the stem of the tree into the plasticene, and the tree looked as if it were growing there.

Then came the hard part. After several disappointing experiments Jane evolved a technique for hanging the tree with ornaments. Painstakingly, she would loop a piece of thin wire about a piece of glass and twist the ends together with a pair of pliers. Then she clipped the wire just above the twist. Next she threaded a fine needle and pushed it cautiously between the wire and the glass. Sometimes the needle broke; and after she had succeeded in getting it through came the worst part of all: knotting the thread securely to the wire at one end, and at the other, knotting it securely to a twig. It was difficult, exasperating work. Jane's fingers felt large and clumsy but gradually they became more skillful.

And the tree was becoming a work of art. Gnarled, yet graceful, it stood in its little green bucket. It was silver-gray, and hanging from its branches, on their almost invisible threads, were the jewels of glass: blue, green, turquoise, lavender.

But she still had nothing for her father. I could bake him a cake, she thought sadly; but her cakes could never be relied on, and he did not care much for sweets in any case.

It was the twenty-third of December; then the twenty-fourth, and still there was nothing.

"Poor Daddy, it will have to be a cake," said Jane, picking up her basket to go collecting for the last time before Christmas. A cold north wind was blowing, and her mother made her wear her winter coat—the first time she had worn it since last year.

It was a brilliant day; the sky a pure and stony blue, the sea blazing with sparks. Far down the beach two winch-trucks were bringing in a seine. Gulls mewed above them.

She shifted the basket handle to her arm and put her cold hands in the pockets of her coat. And what was *this*? Hardly believing, she brought her right hand out and saw that she was holding a quarter.

"Carfare from last year!" cried Jane, giving an involuntary leap in the air. "Jonas! *Jonas!* We've got twenty-five cents to buy a present for Daddy!"

There was a noise of men's voices, and she saw that they had nearly reached the fishermen. On the trucks the winches were turning and the ropes were slowly hauled landward.

"Jo, I have an idea," Jane said quietly, and she walked over to a fat man in a sou'wester who seemed to be the boss.

"Sir?" said Jane.

"Yes, Sis?"

"I would like to buy a fish, " Jane said. "I can pay you twenty-five cents."

"*Twenty-five* ce—Listen, Sis, you know what we get per pound for these stripers at auction? But what'd you want a big fish like that for? A minna'd be a meal for you."

"It's a Christmas present for my father," Jane explained patiently. "He likes fish."

And in the end she had her fish: a fine striped bass that was heavy in the basket. The man had wanted her to take it for nothing, but Jane had insisted on paying him.

At home she hid the fish in the garage so that it would stay cold until she wrapped it.

The next day was a marvelous Christmas. Though the presents were few, they were of excellent quality. Their mother had made candy and cookies and their father had written and illustrated a story for each of them.

Toppy's presents were clay bowls he made at school, one for everybody. They were a great success. And Jane's presents were nearly the most successful of all.

Toppy put the war bonnet on and kept it on, and most of the day he went about the house carrying the green glass buoy and gloating.

Jane had had a terrible time doing up the fish. It did not lend itself well to tissue paper and ribbons, but she had conquered the problem and was rewarded by her father's look, first of shock and then of pleasure, as he unwrapped it.

But the glass tree was the best of all. Her mother set it on the windowsill in the sun-shine and all the gems took light: amethyst, emerald, aquamarine, sapphire.

"Jane, it is the prettiest thing I ever saw," her mother said, and meant it.

After Christmas, Jane went to school and found new friends; she and Toppy learned to skate, went tobogganing on Kettle Neck's one hill, and later discovered the delights of a Kettle Neck spring. But as long as she lived Jane would always remember with special joy the time she had gone to the Atlantic Ocean to do her Christmas shopping.
ELIZABETH ENRIGHT

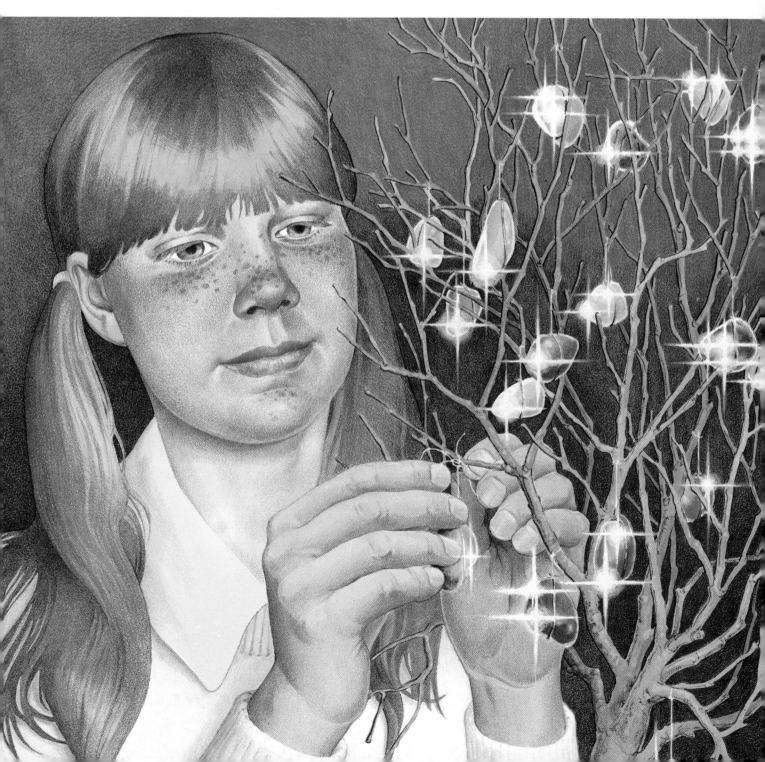

The Tree That Didn't Get Trimmed

I f you walk through a grove of balsam trees you will notice that the young trees are silent; they are listening. But the old, tall ones—especially the firs—are whispering. They are telling the story of The Tree That Didn't Get Trimmed. It sounds like a sad story, and the murmur of the old trees as they tell it is rather solemn; but it is an encouraging story for young saplings to hear. On warm autumn days when the whole forest smells sweet and sad and the hardwood trees are boasting of the gay colors they are beginning to show, many a young evergreen has been cheered by it.

All young fir trees dream of being a Christmas tree some day. With that vision of brightness and gaiety before them they patiently endure

the sharp sting of the ax, the long hours pressed together on a freight car. But every December there are more trees cut down than are needed for Christmas. And that is the story that no one has thought to put down.

The tree in this story should never have been cut. He wouldn't have been, but it was getting dark in the Vermont woods, and the man with the ax said to himself, "Just one more." But cutting young trees with a sharp, beautifully balanced ax is fascinating; you go on and on; there's a sort of cruel pleasure in it. The blade goes through the soft wood with one whistling stroke and the boughs sink down with a swish.

The fir was a fine, well-grown youngster, but too tall for his age; his branches were rather scraggly. If he'd been left there he would have been an unusually big tree some day; but now he was at that awkward age and didn't have the tapering shape and the thick, even foliage that people like on Christmas trees. Worse still, instead of running up to a straight, clean spire, his top was a bit lopsided, with a fork in it.

But he didn't know this as he stood with many others, leaning against the side wall of the greengrocer's shop. In those cold December days he was very happy, thinking of the pleasures to come. He had heard of the delights of Christmas Eve: the stealthy setting-up of the tree, the tinsel balls and colored toys and stars, the peppermint canes and birds with spun-glass tails. Even that old anxiety of Christmas trees—burning candles—did not worry him, for he had been told that nowadays people use strings of tiny electric bulbs which cannot set one on fire. So he looked forward to the festival with a confident heart.

"I shall be very grand," he said. "I hope there will be children to admire me. It must be a great moment when the children hang their stockings on you!" He even felt sorry for the first trees that were chosen and taken away. It would be best, he considered, not to be bought until Christmas Eve. Then, in the shining darkness someone would pick him out, put him carefully along the running board of a car, and away they would go. The tire chains would clack and jingle merrily on the snowy road. He imagined a big house with fire glowing on a hearth; the hushed rustle of wrapping paper and parcels being unpacked. Someone would say, "Oh, what a beautiful tree!" How erect and stiff he would brace himself in his iron tripod stand.

But day after day went by, one by one the other trees were taken, and he began to grow troubled. For everyone who looked at him seemed to have an unkind word. "Too tall," said one lady. "No, this one wouldn't do, the branches are too skimpy," said another. "If I chop off the top," said the greengrocer, "it wouldn't be so bad." The tree shuddered, but the customer had already passed on to look at others. Some of his branches ached where the grocer had bent them upward to make his shape more attractive.

Across the street was a Ten Cent Store. Its bright windows were full of scarlet odds and ends. When the doors opened he could see people crowded along the aisles, cheerfully jostling one another with bumpy packages. A buzz of talk, a shuffle of feet, a constant ringing of cash drawers came noisily out of that doorway. He could see flashes of marvelous color, ornaments for luckier trees. Every evening, as the time drew nearer, the pavements were more thronged. The handsomer trees, not so tall as he but more bushy

and shapely, were ranked in front of him; as they were taken away he could see the gaiety only too well. Then he was shown to a lady who wanted a tree very cheap. "You can have this one for a dollar," said the grocer. This was only one-third of what the grocer had asked for him at first, but even so the lady refused him and went across the street to buy a little artificial tree at the toy store. The man pushed him back carelessly, and he toppled over and fell alongside the wall. No one bothered to pick him up. He was almost glad, for now his pride would be spared.

Now it was Christmas Eve. It was a foggy evening with a drizzling rain; the alley alongside the store was thick with trampled slush. As he lay there among broken boxes and fallen scraps of holly, strange thoughts came to him. In the still Northern forest his wounded stump was already buried in forgetful snow. He remembered the wintry sparkle of the woods, the big trees with crusts and clumps of silver on their broad boughs, the keen singing of the lonely wind. He remembered the strong, warm feeling of his roots reaching down into the safe earth. That is a good feeling; it means to a tree just what it means to you to stretch your toes down toward the bottom of a well-tucked bed. And he had given up all this to lie here, disdained and forgotten, in a littered alley. The splash of feet, the chime of bells, the cry of cars went past him. He trembled a little with self-pity and vexation. "No toys and stockings for me," he thought sadly, and shed some of his needles.

Late that night, after all the shopping was over, the grocer came out to clear away what was left. The boxes, the broken wreaths, the empty barrels, and our tree with one or two

others that hadn't been sold, all were thrown through the side door into the cellar. The door was locked and he lay there in the dark. One of his branches, doubled under him in the fall, ached so he thought it must be broken. "So this is Christmas," he said to himself.

All the next day it was very still in the cellar. There was an occasional creak as one of the bruised trees tried to stretch itself. Feet went along the pavement overhead, and there was a booming of church bells, but everything had a slow, disappointed sound. Christmas is always a little sad, after such busy preparations. The unwanted trees lay on the stone floor, watching the furnace light flicker on a hatchet that had been left there.

The day after Christmas a man came in who wanted some green boughs to decorate a cemetery. The grocer took the hatchet and seized the trees. They were too disheartened to care. Chop, chop, went the blade, and the sweet-smelling branches were carried away. The naked trunks were thrown into a corner.

And now our tree, what was left of him, had plenty of time to think. He no longer could feel anything, for trees feel with their branches, but they think with their trunks. What did he think about as he grew dry and stiff? He thought that it had been silly of him to imagine such a fine, gay career for himself, and he was sorry for other young fir trees, still growing in the fresh, hilly countryside, who were enjoying the same fantastic dreams.

Now perhaps you don't know what happens to the trunks of leftover Christmas trees. You could never guess. Farmers come in from the suburbs and buy them at five cents each for beanpoles and grape arbors. So perhaps (here begins the encouraging part of this story) they are really happier, in the end, than the trees that get trimmed for Santa Claus. They go back into the fresh, moist earth of spring, and when the sun grows hot the quick tendrils of the vines climb up them and presently they are decorated with the red blossoms of the bean or the little blue globes of the grape.

So one day the naked, dusty fir poles were taken out of the cellar, and thrown into a truck with many others, and made a rattling journey out into the country. The farmer unloaded them in his yard and was stacking them up by the barn when his wife came out to watch him.

"There!" she said. "That's just what I want, a nice long pole with a fork in it. Jim, put that one over there to hold up the clothesline." It was the first time that anyone had praised our tree, and his dried-up heart swelled with a tingle of forgotten sap. They put him near one end of the clothesline, with his stump close to a flower bed. The fork that had been despised for a Christmas star was just the thing to hold up a clothesline. It was wash day, and soon the farmer's wife began bringing out the family's wet clothing to swing and freshen in the clean, bright air. And the very first thing that she hung near the top of the Christmas pole was a cluster of her children's clean stockings.

That isn't quite the end of the story, as the old fir trees whisper it in the breeze. The Tree That Didn't Get Trimmed was so cheerful watching the stockings and other gay little clothes that plumped out in the wind that he didn't notice what was going on—or going up—below him. A vine had caught hold of his trunk and was steadily twisting upward. And one morning, when the farmer's wife came out intending to shift him, she stopped and exclaimed. "Why, I mustn't move this pole," she said. "The morning glory has run right up it." So it had, and our bare pole was blue and crimson with color.

Something nice, the old firs believe, always happens to the trees that don't get trimmed. They even believe that some day one of the Christmas-tree beanpoles will be the starting point for another Magic Beanstalk, as in the fairy tale of the boy who climbed up the bean tree and killed the giant. When that happens, fairy tales will begin all over again.
CHRISTOPHER MORLEY

The Party!

What a sparkling day for a party! How peaceful it is in Deep Green Wood! UNTIL. . . the forest comes alive with whoops, chirps, and shouts. Soon the animals burst into the sunny clearing where one beautiful pine tree stands.

"Let's decorate our tree!" cries Ranger Rick.

The animals all pitch in. In a flash, the tree glitters with bright ornaments.

"Cookies!" offers Zelda Possum. Davey Deer's hungry and so is Cubby Bear.

"Hey!" Zelda laughs. "Save enough for the children!"

"When they come," says Rick, "we'll share our *best* present with them."

"*What* best present?" asks Cubby, looking around for a ribbon-tied package.

Rick chuckles. "What's the best present *you* know of?"

Cubby thinks a minute and says, "Why, all of us being together *here.*"

"And just think, Cubby," says Rick. "Our life in Deep Green Wood is nature's gift."

"Hurray for nature!" cries Ollie Otter.

"And hurray for all the *people* who love Deep Green Wood!" hoots Wise Old Owl.

"How lucky we are to have good food and air and water!" says Rick. Then he cups his paw to his ear. "Listen! I hear children's voices!"

All together, they call: "HAPPY HOLIDAYS, KIDS!"

Text Credits

Wise Old Owl's Holiday Traditions

"Nomads of the Far North" (p. 10), reprinted from G. P. Putnam's Sons by permission of the author and Larry Sternig Literary Agency. Copyright © 1976 by Alice L. Hopf.

"Mistletoe Magic" (p. 14), copyright 1976 by the National Wildlife Federation. Reprinted from the December issue of *Ranger Rick's Nature Magazine*.

"The Forever Christmas Tree" (p. 18), condensation of *The Forever Christmas Tree* by Yoshiko Uchida. Text copyright © 1963 by Yoshiko Uchida. Reprinted by permission of Charles Scribner's Sons.

"Your Christmas Tree" (p. 22), copyright 1967 by the National Wildlife Federation. Reprinted from the December issue of *Ranger Rick's Nature Magazine*.

"Bee-utiful Candles" (p. 26), reprinted from *The Pitzel Holiday Book* by Leonard Jaffe, copyright © 1962 by KTAV Publishing House, Inc.

Becky Hare's Winter Wonderland

"Snow" (p. 32), from *Snow* by Thelma Harrington Bell. Copyright 1954 by Thelma Harrington Bell and Corydon Bell. Adapted by permission of Viking Penguin Inc.

"What Do You Know About Snow?" (p. 35), copyright 1967 by the National Wildlife Federation. Reprinted from the February issue of *Ranger Rick's Nature Magazine*.

"Monsters in the Ice" (p. 36), reprinted by permission of G. P. Putnam's Sons from *Great Mysteries of the Earth* by Charles Hapgood. Copyright © 1960 by Charles Hapgood.

"When Winter Comes" (p. 38), copyright 1975 by the National Wildlife Federation. Reprinted from the December issue of *Ranger Rick's Nature Magazine*.

"Tale of the Grouse" (p. 42), copyright 1975 by the National Wildlife Federation. Reprinted from the February issue of *Ranger Rick's Nature Magazine*.

"Naput and Nanook" (p. 44), copyright 1974 by the National Wildlife Federation. Reprinted from the December issue of *Ranger Rick's Nature Magazine*.

Sammy Squirrel's Winter Adventures

"Warm Tips for Winter Trips" (p. 50), copyright 1973 by the National Wildlife Federation. Adapted from "Six Tricks for a Warm Winter" in the December issue of *Ranger Rick's Nature Magazine*.

"Walk in the Winter Woods" (p. 52), copyright 1972 by the National

Illustration Credits

Cover: Ranger Rick and friends caroling, Lorin Thompson. Page 1: Ranger Rick with gift, Lorin Thompson. 2-3: Ranger Rick and friends sledding, Lorin Thompson. 4-5: Ranger Rick and friends in Deep Green Wood, Lorin Thompson. 6-7: Map of Deep Green Wood, Lorin Thompson.

Wise Old Owl's Holiday Traditions

Page 8: Wise Old Owl, Lorin Thompson. 8-9: Child decorating tree, Kent and Donna Dannen. 11: Caribou herd on snow-covered slope, Entheos. Caribou calf sleeping, Fred Bruemmer. 12: Caribou calf foraging on tundra, Bill Ruth. Caribou herd migrating across river, George W. Calef. 12-13: Caribou bucks battling, Bill Ruth. 14: Mistletoe with blue jay, Druid and children, Ted Lewin. 15: Sprig of mistletoe, Ted Lewin. 17: Poinsettias, Gene Ahrens/ Bruce Coleman, Inc. Christmas rose, Jane Burton/Bruce Coleman, Inc. Holly, Jane Burton/Bruce Coleman, Inc. Rosemary, Jane Burton/Bruce Coleman, Inc. Ivy, Wendy W. Cortesi. Sweet bay (laurel), Jane Burton/ Bruce Coleman, Inc. 18-19: Boy with dog, Hsien-Min Yang. 20-21: Family by decorated tree, Hsien-Min Yang. 22: Horse-drawn sled, Richard W. Brown. 23: Pine, fir, spruce and juniper branches, Davis Meltzer. 25: Saint Nicholas Day, Swiss National Tourist Office. Santa Lucia Day, Fred Ward/Black Star. Hanukkah, Nathan Benn/Woodfin Camp, Inc. 27: Hummingbird and children, Roz Schanzer. 28: Queen bee and children, Roz Schanzer.

Becky Hare's Winter Wonderland

Page 30: Becky Hare, Lorin Thompson. 30-31: Deer in snow, Erwin and Peggy Bauer. 32: Boy throwing snowball, Phoebe Dunn-DPI/Natural History. 33: Snowflakes (top and bottom), Buffalo Museum of Science. Snowflake (middle), Roger J. Cheng, State University of New York at Albany. 34: Avalanche, Art Twomey/ The Image Bank. 35: Snow experiments, Roz Schanzer. 36-37: Men, dog and mammoth, Ted Lewin. 38-39: Ox and snowy owl, Charles Harper. 40: Ladybird beetles and rattlesnakes, Charles Harper. 41: Monarch butterflies and mountain quail, Charles Harper. 42: Ruffed grouse and great horned owl, Tony Chen. 42-43: Snowy scene with wildlife, Tony Chen. 44-45: Polar bears and boy, Ted Lewin. 47: Polar bear and boy, Ted Lewin.

Sammy Squirrel's Winter Adventures

Page 48: Sammy Squirrel, Lorin Thompson. 48-49: Children and snowman, © Michael Philip Manheim 1975. 50: Children sledding, Clyde H. Smith. 50-51: Penguin, Cyndy Szekeres. 51: Penguin, Cyndy Szekeres. 52: Child in snow, Laurence Pringle. Mountain laurel, John Shaw. 53: Maple leaf, William S. Weems/ Woodfin Camp, Inc. Holly, Linda Bartlett/Woodfin Camp, Inc. Lilac buds, Robert P. Carr. English ivy, Jane Burton/Bruce Coleman, Inc. 55: Snowshoe hare, John Shaw. Tree stripped of bark, Jack Dermid. Evening grosbeak, Kent and Donna

Wildlife Federation. Reprinted from the January issue of *Ranger Rick's Nature Magazine*.

"Who Went There?" (p. 56), copyright 1972 by the National Wildlife Federation. Adapted from "Animal Tracks" in the January issue of *Ranger Rick's Nature Magazine*.

"Crystal Castle" (p. 58), adapted from *Outdoor Art for Kids* by Charleen Kinser. Copyright © 1975 by Charleen Kinser. Used by permission of Follett Publishing Company, a division of Follett Corporation.

"Skiing Through Winter" (p. 60), copyright 1972 by the National Wildlife Federation. Originally appeared as "XCS" in the December issue of *Ranger Rick's Nature Magazine*.

Ollie Otter's Fun Pages

"Ornaments from Many Lands" (p. 64), concept and models by

Peter Hamilton Kent.

"Light Up Your Holidays" (p. 66), concept and models by Peter Hamilton Kent.

"Tasty Trimmings" (p. 68), concept and finished cookies by Merrill Clift.

"Reindeer Puppets" (p. 72), concept and models by Peter Hamilton Kent.

"Stamp-Out Wrappings" (p. 74), copyright 1979 by the National Wildlife Federation. Adapted from "Stamp Out Art" in the December issue of *Ranger Rick's Nature Magazine*.

Ranger Rick's Christmas Eve Stories

"The Little Old Lady Who Liked Spiders" (p. 78), used by permission of Eileen Snyder.

"The Sea Christmas" (p. 82), reprinted by permission of Russell & Volkening, Inc., as agents for the author. Copyright © 1965 by Elizabeth Enright.

"The Tree That Didn't Get Trimmed" (p. 86), adaptation of "The Tree That Didn't Get Trimmed" from *Essays* by Christopher Morley (J. B. Lippincott Co.). Copyright 1925, 1927 by Christopher Morley. By permission of Harper & Row, Publishers, Inc.

Dannen. Fox squirrel, Jon Farrar. 56: Red fox, Brian Milne. Mouse tracks, Grant Heilman. Deer tracks, Wilfried D. Schurig. Opossum tracks, Jack Dermid. 57: Rabbit tracks, Grant Heilman. Bobwhite tracks, Jack Dermid. Duck tracks, Jack Dermid. Beaver track, Len Rue, Jr. Hare tracks, Wilfried D. Schurig. River otter tracks, Jack Dermid. 58: Ice castle molds, Verlin Miller. 59: Crystal castle, Verlin Miller. 60: Ski binding, Hanson Carroll. 61: Family in snow, family skiing, and boy on skis, Hanson Carroll.

Ollie Otter's Fun Pages

Page 62: Ollie Otter, Lorin Thompson. 62-63: Reindeer cookie, Leah Bendavid-Val (NWF). 64: German snowflake and Scandinavian wood ornaments, Leah Bendavid-Val (NWF). 65: Ukrainian cobweb, Mexican yarn animal, Polish star and tree decorated with ornaments, Leah Bendavid-Val (NWF). 66-67: Iceberg candles, tin candleholders and luminarios, Leah Bendavid-Val (NWF).

68: Lamb and raccoon cookies, Leah Bendavid-Val (NWF). 69: Children combining cookie ingredients, Leah Bendavid-Val (NWF). 70: Shaping and decorating cookies, Leah Bendavid-Val (NWF). 71: Rabbit and camel cookies and decorated tree, Leah Bendavid-Val (NWF). 72-73: Reindeer puppets, Leah Bendavid-Val (NWF). 74-75: Children decorating gift wrapping papers, Leah Bendavid-Val (NWF).

Ranger Rick's Christmas Eve Stories

Page 76: Ranger Rick, Lorin Thompson. 76-77: House with Christmas lights, Harald Sund/The Image Bank. 78: Little old lady with spiders, Trina Schart Hyman. 79: Little old lady with Christmas tree, Trina Schart Hyman. 80: Spiders, Trina Schart Hyman. 81: Little old lady with web-decorated tree, Trina Schart Hyman. 82: Starfish, Carol Smith. 83: Girl and dog on beach, Carol Smith. 85: Girl decorating tree, Carol Smith. 86-87: Man chopping down tree, Lynne Cherry. 89: Tree

in alley, Lynne Cherry. 90-91: Woman hanging clothes on line, Lynne Cherry.

The Party!

Pages 92-93: The party, Lorin Thompson.

Library of Congress Cataloging in Publication Data

Main entry under title:

Ranger Rick's holiday book.

Articles from Ranger Rick's nature magazine and other sources, plus original materials.

SUMMARY: Presents information about plants, animals, and nature in winter; examines various holiday traditions; and gives directions for making such objects as ice sculpture, toys, and cookies. Includes Christmas stories.

1. Christmas—Juvenile literature.
2. Winter—Juvenile literature.
[1. Christmas. 2. Winter] I. National Wildlife Federation. II. Ranger Rick's nature magazine.
GT4985.R26   394.2'683   80-81621
ISBN 0-912186-38-0

National Wildlife Federation

1412 16th Street, N.W.
Washington, D.C.
20036

Thomas L. Kimball, *Executive Vice President*
J. A. Brownridge, *Administrative Vice President*
James D. Davis, *Director, Book Development*

Staff for this Book

Elizabeth G. Jones
Editor

Victor H. Waldrop
Art Editor

Jane D'Alelio
Designer

Robyn Gregg
Editorial Assistant

Priscilla Sharpless
Production Manager

Mariam Thayer Rutter
Production Artist

Cathy Pelletier
Permissions Editor

Acknowledgments

The editors of *Ranger Rick's Nature Magazine* are old hands at helping children to enjoy wildlife as part of their winter holiday festivities. The editorial staff for this book appreciate their letting us use some of their fine articles and send special thanks to Donna Miller, design director of the magazine, for help in planning the illustrations.

We are also happy to have had an author of the adventures of Ranger Rick and his friends, Bet Hennefrund, write the main introduction, the introductory paragraphs for each chapter, and the rousing description of "The Party!"

We are grateful for support from many of our colleagues at the National Wildlife Federation, in particular Craig Tufts, naturalist, for reviewing the biological content of the articles. For their interest and technical assistance with this book, we are also indebted to many friends at the Smithsonian Museum of Natural History; to Margaret N. Coughlan of the Library of Congress Children's Literature Center; and to the staffs of the Library of Congress and the Public Library of Fairfax, Virginia.